HOW TO STA... ...
BUSINESS

BONUS MATERIAL

Are included with this book:

- Workbook
- Book Summary
- *Building Authority and Credibility* (PDF)
- Guide to Setting up HostGator and WordPress.org
- Guide to Setting up Google Analytics
- List Of WordPress Plugins
- Other Useful Resources

You can find the link to download them at the end of the book (see table of content).

Copyright © 2016 by Emilie Pelletier

All rights reserved. No part of this publication may be reproduced, distributed, or transmitted in any form or by any means, including photocopying, recording, or other electronic or mechanical methods, without the prior written permission of the author, except in the case of brief quotations embodied in critical reviews and certain other noncommercial uses permitted by copyright law.

Disclaimer

This disclaimer governs the use of this book. By using this book, you accept this disclaimer in full.

The book contains information about entrepreneurship, business and marketing-related topics.

Although I have made every effort to ensure that the information in this book was correct at press time, I do not assume and hereby disclaim any liability to any party for any loss, damage, or disruption caused by errors or omissions, whether such errors or omissions result from negligence, accident, or any other cause.

Without prejudice to the generality of the foregoing paragraph, I do not represent, warrant, undertake or guarantee:

- That the information in the eBook is correct, accurate, complete or non-misleading;
- That the use of the guidance in the eBook will lead to any particular outcome or result;
- Or In particular, that by using the guidance in the eBook you will build a successful online business.

In this disclaimer, "I" means (and "my" refer to) the author of this book, Emilie Pelletier.

Table of Content

BECOMING AN ONLINE ENTREPRENEUR 1

CHOOSING A BUSINESS MODEL 5

FINDING YOUR BUSINESS IDEA 14

CHOOSING A NICHE MARKET: YOUR *IDEAL* CUSTOMERS 25

CONNECTING WITH YOUR AUDIENCE 42

DEFINING YOUR BRAND 56

GETTING PAST THE TECHNICAL ASPECTS 79

BUILDING YOUR EMAIL LIST 88

GETTING TRAFFIC TO YOUR WEBSITE 112

STARTING TO GENERATE REVENUE 156

SETTING A PRICE FOR YOUR PRODUCT 174

CONVINCING POTENTIAL CUSTOMERS 188

GETTING FEEDBACK THROUGH TESTING 203

OUTSOURCING 214

WHAT'S NEXT? 219

HAVE YOU ENJOYED THIS BOOK? 222

BONUS MATERIAL 223

COMPLEMENTARY READING 224

INTRODUCTION

BECOMING AN ONLINE ENTREPRENEUR

The Entrepreneurial Spirit

Imagine working for yourself, with no one to tell you what to do. You take on the projects that appeal to you most, and feel proud as you watch them grow and add value to the market. If this sounds more interesting to you than working for an employer, then you likely have an *entrepreneurial spirit*.

Perhaps you've always wanted to be your own boss, but have never started your own business due to a lack of time, money, or even ideas. Maybe you were held back by the fear of putting yourself—or your family—at risk.

However, it has never been as easy to become an entrepreneur as it is today. The Internet has brought down most of the entrance barriers to entrepreneurship. You can start building your business while still working at your regular job and only investing one hour of your time per day. Plus, you have access to a massive gold mine of information to help you succeed: podcasts, books, blogs, etc. You can take advantage of listening to others' experiences, and use this knowledge to build your project faster and safer. What you need most is a deep commitment to learning and the willingness to put some effort into achieving your goals.

The Digital Opportunity

What's so special about an online business?

The cost of starting and operating an online business is minimal, as is the financial risk factor. All you need to purchase are a hosting service (about $5/month) and a domain (about $10/year). For the rest, it all depends on the type of market or service you're getting into, but it *is* possible to start with as little as $100. Pretty incredible, right?

With an online business, you also have the ability to work from wherever you want, whether it be your home, a cafe or a co-working space. You can choose where to live—in your home town or elsewhere—and you have the freedom to organize your schedule almost entirely as you wish.

No, you *won't* have to be stuck in a cubicle all day long, eat lunch at the office cafeteria, spend hours in traffic during rush hour, hit the gym at the same time as everyone else and wait in line for the next available treadmill. Perhaps most importantly, your salary *won't* be limited to what an employer is willing to provide.

The Perfect Business

In the early 1970s, finance writer Richard Russell penned an article entitled *The Perfect Business.*[1] According to Russell, an ideal business:

- Requires minimal labor
- Sells to the world rather than a single neighborhood
- Has the lowest overhead costs and capital investments

---

[1] *The Perfect Business* DowTheoryLetters.com

- Generates an income that is not limited to your personal output (is passive)
- Allows you more free time
- Is portable or easily moveable (location-independent)
- Satisfies your intellectual and emotional needs (provides fulfillment)

Does this sound like a professional paradise? It was probably difficult to come up with a business idea that corresponded to all of these criteria in the 1970s, but today, with the Internet, it's easily achievable!

There are many ways to make a living online: monetizing a blog, offering consulting or coaching through Skype or Google Hangouts, creating and selling online courses, self-publishing eBooks, joining affiliate programs or selling physical products through an e-commerce store. There are unlimited possibilities, and we'll explore the most popular and rewarding ones later in this book.

The Online Business Blueprint

In this book, I have compiled all of the information about starting a successful online business that I've collected over time so it can serve others. The book will take you step-by-step through the different aspects you should consider when building an online business in order to increase your chances of success. The information is presented in a logical sequence, with each chapter leading to the next. The concepts are not to be taken lightly; I can assure you that seriously considering them as you build your business will save you time in the long run.

This is a book that I wish I would have read a few years ago. I now use this same framework for all of my projects, even in the writing of this book. Of course, all businesses are different, and not all questions can be answered in a single book, but this does provide a solid framework to help you plan your project.

One last thing: In the many examples that will be given in the following chapters, consider how you could use them in *your* field. As Andrew Lock, online marketer, mentions in his book *Big Lessons from Big Brands*: "The real magic happens when you think, *'How can I adapt this concept for my business?'*" That's a crucial part of creativity: using what is already there to construct something new. While building your business, keep your eyes open and stay curious about what others say or do. Paying attention to the dynamic world around you will help to develop new ideas.

Just To Clarify

Some people want to start an Internet business with the primary goal of making a lot of money. Others do it for the lifestyle and freedom that an online business can provide. Before you start your venture, you should ask yourself a very important question: *What is my primary goal in becoming an online entrepreneur?*

This book is about building something valuable for both yourself and others. Although money is a result that comes along with a successful business, this book is written for those craving fulfillment *first*. There are no quick money schemes here. First and foremost, an entrepreneur is a person that creates value. As Jim Rohn would say:

"You get paid for the value you bring to the market."

CHAPTER 1

CHOOSING A BUSINESS MODEL

Which business model should you choose?

Before we get started, there's one important point to clarify: *There is a difference between working on a personal project and building a business.*

When you're working on a personal project, you're doing something that you enjoy for yourself, without asking others what they think. Essentially, it's all about you. When you're building a business, however, it's not all about you anymore; it's about *them*. It's about serving an audience, a market, and responding to a need that they have expressed.

Of course, you should also enjoy what you're doing! However, in the case of a business, enjoying yourself isn't enough. The primary responsibility of a business is to serve the market.

Also, if you create a travel blog, is your blog a business? The answer isn't a simple "yes" or "no." A blog in itself is a personal project, but once you monetize a blog by adding advertising, or by selling your own or an affiliate's products, then you have started a business.

Online Business Models and Website Monetization

There are four main approaches when discussing online business models.

1) Selling your product through your platform (website)
2) Selling others' products on your platform—and getting a commission
3) Having others sell your product—and giving them a commission
4) Selling others' products on a third-party platform—for example, reselling products that aren't yours on Amazon or eBay—and making a profit

The most viable and safe approach, in the long run, is to create your own platform and build your own audience. The most lucrative model within that approach—and the one that will grant you the most control—is to sell your own products or services. The approach that would give you the least control over your income is the fourth one, selling other people's products through a third-party platform. However, these models are not mutually exclusive, and you should use more than one method to generate revenue.

Ramit Sethi, author of the personal finance book *I Will Teach You To Be Rich*, classified the main online business models according to their investment costs and profitability.

Low cost and low profitability:
- Advertising
- Affiliates

High cost and high profitability:
- Software
- Physical products

Low cost and high profitability:
- Consulting
- Online courses

You've probably already guessed that he recommends choosing the "low cost and high profitability" options.

Within the "low cost and high profitability" models, there is one *big* winner: online courses.

Why are online courses better than consulting? Because consulting or coaching implies working one-on-one, which is a direct exchange of your time for money that requires continuous work. On the other hand, online courses can be created once, sold to many people, and they don't require much extra work after they've been produced. They generate passive income. Therefore, according to Ramit Sethi, creating online courses is the most lucrative online business model that you can choose.

Personally, I believe it's good to diversify your income sources and choose more than one way to generate revenue. For example, you could use a mixture of selling your own products and those of affiliates, or offer online courses in addition to your coaching or consulting services. Note that when Ramit refers to online *courses*, eBooks and other information products also qualify.

Here's an overview of the main online business models:

1. Freelancing

If you have a particular skill—like copywriting, video editing, or web designing—you can offer your expertise and get hired through platforms like *Upwork.com*, *Freelancer.com*, *Guru.com*, or even through your personal website.

The downside of freelancing is that even if you are location-independent (can work from home or anywhere), you're still trading your time for money. Unless the work you do is very highly paid and you don't need to work too many hours to generate sufficient income, you might not achieve the lifestyle freedom you're aiming for.

2. Online Consulting

If you're a coach or have a certain type of expertise, you can sell online consulting services over the phone or via a system like Skype.

Keep in mind, however, that the same thing is true for online consulting as for freelancing—you're directly trading your time for money. However, since private consulting is usually very well paid, you might not need many clients to live well.

3. Creating and Selling Your Own Digital Products

As previously mentioned, this is usually the business model that generates the highest revenues. The most common products sold online include eBooks, audio tracks and online courses. You can sell them on your own website, through other people's networks, or through platforms like *Gumroad.com*.

4. Affiliate Marketing

Affiliate marketing is a partnership between a business that has a product to sell and another business that agrees to promote that same product in exchange for a commission.

Affiliate programs can be used in two ways:

1) Recommending other people's products to your own audience and receiving a commission for each sale you make. This can work very well if you already have an audience that trusts you and you have built an email list (we'll talk about the email list in chapter 7).

2) Letting others sell your own product, and offering them a commission for each sale they make. If you have the expertise or knowledge needed to create a good product, then creating such partnerships is an effective way to increase your sales, since you'll reach a larger audience. It's also a good method to expand your brand awareness.

Generally, affiliate commissions for digital products vary between 40% and 75%. Why such a high percentage? Because once created, digital products don't cost anything to reproduce. Thus, for the product initiator, this means generating extra sales at no extra cost.

Affiliates can be a great way to generate a significant income. It's a very genuine form of advertising, since you only recommend products that you sincerely believe your audience will benefit from.

5. Donation

You could even ask your website visitors to give a voluntary donation.

If you provide incredible value and have built an audience of real fans, they may agree to contribute to your site by giving a donation.

You simply have to add a donation button to your page that visitors can click on and enter their payment details. To help you set this system up, *PayPal.com* has a step-by-step guide for creating such a button. One blogger who has been using this method is Maria Popova, at *BrainPickings.org*.

6. Sponsored Articles

If another entrepreneur shares the same target audience, but offers products or services that are complementary to yours (not in direct competition), he or she could write an article on your blog subtly presenting his/her company or product. The other entrepreneur can pay you for the opportunity to expose his/her brand to your audience.

7. Membership Websites

In this case, the buyer (member) pays a recurring fee to have access to information, a product or a service. One thing to consider with such a business model is that it requires you to constantly add new content to justify the recurring cost. I personally believe that it's easier to start by creating single products before considering launching a membership site, which is more work.

8. Forums

Most forums are free to access, but some are private and require a fee to join. This business model is built around the value of being part of a community. Forums can take a significant amount of time to build and attract enough members to generate considerable income.

9. Live Online Events

These can be very lucrative. They can take the form of short webinars, usually one to three hours, or longer events that can last a few days.

These events are the online version of a workshop or an entire convention. They are less expensive to attend and to organize—as they require less logistics—than traditional offline events. Their virtual nature also makes it easier for attendees and speakers from all around the world to participate.

Webinars are typically free to attend and are used as an opportunity to introduce a premium (paid) product. They usually teach something useful, but at an incomplete level, so people are then encouraged to buy the paid service for a better result or in order to have access to all the relevant information. However, some webinars do require a fee to attend.

10. Brokerage

Brokers connect buyers to sellers and facilitate transactions. Some companies in this category are *eBay, Priceline, Expedia, Amazon, PayPal, Craigslist, Airbnb,* and *Fiverr.com*.

Brokers are basically connectors. Choosing this type of business model means creating an exchange platform and receiving commissions for transactions or simply charging a fee to the seller and/or buyer.

11. Sponsorship

Sponsorship is a type of advertising in which one gives money in exchange for exposure and visibility.

For example, the most popular podcasters generate revenues for their show through sponsors. They mention the show sponsors during the episodes and give them increased visibility. This is also a business model that is often used with live events.

12. Advertising

Another business model involves renting advertising space on your website to businesses that have a specific message for your audience.

When you're just starting, the simplest way to do this is to use third-party advertising platforms. These serve as intermediaries between advertisers and site owners. As a site owner, you set up an account with the third-party ad platform, place ads on your website, and collect revenues based on ad impressions or clicks. The downside to this method is that you give up some revenue to the third-party service provider.

The most common ad platform used for this method is *Google AdSense*. It's very easy to set up—simply create an account and follow the directions. To maximize the effectiveness of this business model, you should choose to display contextual ads—ads relevant to the topic of your site. You can select this option in your *AdSense* account.

You could also sell ad space directly to businesses. This method will generate higher revenues, since you don't need to share with an intermediary. However, you need a significant presence for this option and considerable traffic to attract advertisers.

Advertising can be an interesting model if your site gets a lot of traffic. However, since it's rarely a sufficient source of income by itself, it's usually used as a complement to another business model.

What to Remember about these Business Models

1) There is a difference between working on a personal project and building a business—the former is for you, and the latter serves an audience.

2) There are several ways to make money online:
- Freelancing
- Offering online consultation and coaching
- Creating and selling your own products
- Enrolling in an affiliate program
- Asking for a donation
- Accepting sponsored articles on your blog
- Creating a membership or subscription-based website
- Creating a paid forum
- Holding webinars and longer live events
- Finding sponsors
- Using advertising either through *Google AdSense* or by renting ad space directly to companies on your website

CHAPTER 2

FINDING YOUR BUSINESS IDEA

Many individuals *do* want to start a business and become their own bosses, but one of the main barriers that hold them back is their uncertainty regarding *what* business to start. Not knowing where to start, most people choose to stay in the environment they know—their current job.

However, if you really *do* want to become an online entrepreneur, you should know that finding an idea isn't so hard. A business idea usually results from this equation:

A topic you're interested in + People you like and want to help + A problem these people have + A solution you can provide to the problem, which you'll package into a product or service in the format of your choice (book, video, course, etc.).

If you already have a business idea, you'll simply need to validate it. We'll discuss this aspect later in the book. That being said, if you haven't found an idea yet, this is the time to start questioning yourself. The first step is to reflect on your interests and the lifestyle you would like to attain, as well on your natural strengths and the skill set you already possess.

1. What do you dislike about your current job and lifestyle? What would you like to change?

There must be something, or even many things, that you dislike about your current situation. Maybe it's a lack of free time, your commute to work, being told what to do, the nature of the tasks you are required to execute, or insufficient income.

It's important to define what you are trying to escape from so you avoid recreating it in your new lifestyle. For example, if a lack of time is a major issue, then you shouldn't opt for a business model that will require an equal amount of your time (like freelancing, for example). Instead, you should choose a model that generates a passive income.

2. What do you appreciate about your current situation and would like to maintain?

Not everything is necessarily wrong with your current situation. Maybe you enjoy the relationships with your colleagues and working in a team. You probably appreciate not having to think about work once you've clocked out.

It's good to know what you like in order to reproduce it in your online business. For example, even if being a web entrepreneur mainly means working by yourself, there are ways to add social occasions to your new entrepreneurial life. You could share a working space with other entrepreneurs and freelancers, which is now a common practice. You could also attend Meetup groups (MeetUp.com) in your field and occasionally meet with other like-minded entrepreneurs.

3. What are your main interests?

There are topics and activities that are naturally more appealing to you than others. You feel more enthusiastic about certain conversation topics, and are more curious to learn about some subjects. If you're planning on creating a blog—or even if you aren't—think of a topic that you could write about every day, without growing bored or lacking inspiration. Also, answer these questions:

- When you enter a bookstore, which section do you head to first?
- Which kind of magazines do you read while waiting at the dentist?
- Which TV channels do you watch?
- Which sections of the newspaper do you like to read?
- Which classes did you enjoy most in school?
- Which activities do you engage in during your free time?
- Which websites do you like browsing?

It's obviously important to choose a topic that you're interested in, since it will become a part of your daily life. Otherwise, you will eventually get bored, sometimes sooner rather than later.

It's important to note that, over time, you might discover that your interests are slightly different than what you initially thought. Sometimes, there are activities that you enjoy as a hobby, but not necessarily as a job.

The first website I started was about leading a healthy lifestyle; nutrition, fitness and stress management were the main topics. I loved reading about these topics and felt the desire to share the useful information that I was learning with others. A few months into my project, though, I realized that I genuinely disliked researching scientific data about nutrition and other health-related topics. Writing the blog wasn't enjoyable at all, and daily writing soon turned into weekly writing, and then monthly writing... Something similar could happen to you. I recommend that you start exploring a topic and write about it for a few weeks to see how it feels before choosing that subject for your business project.

If you can't think of something that interests you, then it's time to explore. Go out and try new activities, attend events or learn a new skill. Think of something you have always been curious about, and talk to people already engaged in that activity. Also, be curious about the people you meet. Ask them about their jobs, their interests, and their projects. It might be uncomfortable at first, but it will definitely help you generate new ideas.

A good book full of inspiring entrepreneurial stories is *The $100 Startup*, by Chris Guillebeau. It's not only about online businesses, but it recounts the stories of individuals who have managed to make a living from their passion.

4. What are your natural talents and strengths?

We're not talking about skills quite yet. Natural talents and strengths are not necessarily abilities that you've gained through practice and experience; they are activities that naturally come easier for you than for others. You might be very good at writing and playing with words, performing manual tasks, solving problems, or analyzing concepts.

If you aren't sure of what your natural strengths are, I suggest you read the excellent book written by Tom Rath, *Strengths Finder 2.0*. It comes with a test, which can give you great insight into your natural abilities.

5. What are your "natural" weaknesses?

Be careful not to think of a weakness as a lack of skills, because skills can be learned. Your "natural" weaknesses are aspects with which you feel less at ease. For example, maybe you don't have a well-developed sense of aesthetics or struggle with organization.

We should all adopt a growth mindset and a desire to constantly work on our weaknesses to improve ourselves, but it's still wise to acknowledge what comes naturally easy for us, so we don't pick a business model that will make things unnecessarily hard at the beginning.

6. What's your personality like?

Certain aspects of your personality will determine which contexts will bring you more joy and fulfillment than others, in the same way that your strengths and natural talents will.

An easy example to illustrate the role that personality plays is to consider the difference between an introvert and an extrovert. An extrovert is more likely to enjoy networking events and social gatherings than an introvert, whereas an introvert probably won't mind spending many hours working alone. A shy person might feel uncomfortable being in front of the camera. Someone active will probably prefer to move around a lot, rather than sit in front of a computer several hours each day.

7. What are your skills, experience, and expertise?

Other elements to keep in mind are your skills and expertise. These are the abilities and knowledge that you have acquired over time at work and through other activities.

Starting your business around your current skills and expertise will definitely help you move faster in the process, since you won't have to spend too much time acquiring related knowledge. However, it's not mandatory to be an expert, nor even very experienced. Don't forget that you can always learn. Like Tim Ferriss, author of the bestseller, *The 4-Hour Workweek*, says:

"To sell information products—books, courses, etc.— you only need to know a little more than some people."

To learn more about how to accelerate your learning process and build authority in your field, I encourage you to read the document about gaining expertise in the bonus material section.

8. Who is working in the field?

What kind of people work in the field you're thinking of choosing? Would you like to interact and connect with them? This may seem trivial, but it's much more enjoyable to be surrounded by—and build relationships with—like-minded people.

9. Find a niche topic.

Once you've found a topic that you're interested in—for example, photography—you'll need to get more specific as to which aspect of the topic you want to cover. We call this "niching down your topic."

A *niche topic* is a narrower category within your topic, such as *outdoor* photography, versus *general* photography. Choosing a niche topic versus a broader topic will increase the chances of your business being successful, because competition won't be as prevalent. Starting a business around a very broad topic is a common mistake made by new entrepreneurs. It's very difficult to compete for attention and market share with companies that are already well established. By choosing a narrower, more specific topic, you will increase your chances of standing out and getting noticed. You'll also build your authority in the field and generate revenues faster.

Dorie Clark, a branding expert, provides a good example to illustrate this idea:

Let's say that you're an online marketer interested in social media. There are already many well-established social media experts, which makes the sphere quite competitive. Instead of trying to compete against well-known experts, you could choose another tactic. You could decide to become an expert in a *newer social platform*, like Periscope. Dorie Clark says that if you were to write one blog post about a different aspect of Periscope every day for 60 days, at the end of that period, you could be seen as a Periscope "expert," since few people will have explored the same topic in such detail. Once you have established your authority and your credibility as a Periscope expert, you could choose to expand your field of expertise to other social media.

If you aren't sure which topic to pick, you could always consider one within these proven-to-be-profitable categories:

- Health and well-being
- Personal development
- Dating
- Business and finance

There will always be space to enter one of these topic markets, since they correspond to needs that many people want to satisfy or common problems they wish to solve. You could easily choose a specific aspect (niche) within one of these broad categories. For example—losing pregnancy weight, dating for seniors, paying back student loans or overcoming a fear of public speaking.

Finally, to help you get through this introspection, and define what you really want, a good exercise is to visualize your ideal working day, ideal week, and ideal year. Consider this: "If money wasn't a factor, how would I like to spend my days?" Then, try to find a way to generate an income that is close to that ideal.

One last thing: Taking a look at businesses that others have started can help you develop your own ideas. If you browse the Internet and search for topics you like and add the term "business" or even "online business" along with the topic in the search field, you'll almost certainly find examples of what others have done. For example, if you look for "photography online business," you'll find many different types of online photography businesses.

The inspiring stories of people who have successfully started all kinds of businesses are also great resources, and are readily available by listening to podcasts. This can help you to consider many opportunities that you wouldn't have even thought of before.

Podcasts are free to download from the iTunes store; some of the best business-related Podcasts include *The School Of Greatness*, *The Side Hustle Show*, *Entrepreneur On Fire*, and *The Smart Passive Income*.

What to Remember about Finding a Business Idea

1) It's important to choose a topic that you're interested in.

2) It's better to choose a niche (narrow) topic.

3) You could always consider a niche topic within these proven-to-be-profitable categories:

- Health and well-being
- Personal development
- Dating
- Business and finance

Take Action

(Suggested time to allow for the exercise: 2 hours)

1) On a piece of paper, write down the answers to the following questions:

- What would you change about your current situation?
- What would you keep about your current situation?
- What are your main interests?
- What are your natural talents and strengths?
- What are your natural weaknesses?
- What are your strong personality traits (for example, are you more of an introvert or an extrovert)?
- What skills, experience, and expertise have you acquired through work and other activities?
- What do you have enough expertise in to write an eBook? Or, if you were to write an eBook, what would you like to write about?

2) Visualize your ideal day, month, and year.

3) Brainstorm possible ways to monetize your topic of choice using different business models.

4) Browse the web, look for what already exists, and listen to business podcasts to give you more ideas.

CHAPTER 3

CHOOSING A NICHE MARKET: YOUR *IDEAL* CUSTOMERS

What's a Niche Market?

We've already mentioned the term *niche*—which basically means "more specific"—and the importance of choosing a niche topic for your business.

When we say niche *market* versus niche *topic,* we are referring to the people to whom you're trying to sell your product, not to the product itself. You introduce your product or service to your target market. They are your potential audience, clients, or buyers.

Your market = Your audience (or potential clients or customers)

In marketing, we use the term *mass markets* and *niche markets* to describe how broad or specific the group of people we are trying to reach to sell our product or service is. A *mass market* is very broad, meaning almost everyone, while a *niche* is narrow, representing a smaller group of people who share distinct characteristics.

These characteristics are usually related to demographic *and* psychographic traits, including interests, behavior, background and context, as well as the goal or end result this target audience is trying to achieve. For example, let's consider two individuals looking to hire a photographer. One is a mother who wants pictures of her newborn baby, and the other is a young professional who needs a few portraits for his business profile. Both are looking for a professional photographer, but for very different reasons. Not only do these two individuals belong to distinctive demographic groups, but they are also driven by different motives. They should be considered as comprising two different market *niches*. Thus, within broad markets, you can find many sub-markets, or niches.

What Does This Mean for You?

Mark McGuiness, business consultant for creative people (*LateralAction.com*), says:

"You are not creating products or services for everyone. You are creating them for the discerning ones—the ones with the particular needs—or tastes—you can satisfy, or the very specialist problems you can solve."

That's exactly what the concept of a niche is—targeting the people predisposed to being pleased by what you have to offer, and *excluding* all others in your marketing efforts.

Know Your Target Market Before Creating a Product

To increase the probability of your business's success, choosing a market should come before creating a product.

Many businesses do the opposite. They create a product and then attempt to push it into the market through advertising and by trying to persuade people to buy it. This method often fails. The more efficient way to build a business is to choose a market first, and find out what the needs of that specific market are, before creating customized products in response to those needs.

This is much more effective when you follow this sequence:

1. Choose a market.

2. Find the needs of that market.

3. Create products that solve the market's problems (needs).

Should Everyone Choose a Niche Market Instead of a Mass Market?

The answer is *yes*. It's usually best not to "pitch" to *everyone*.

However, that does raise the question of how narrow your market should be. Generally, for an online business, you have the advantage of being as narrow as possible (by "possible," I mean as long as you have a large enough potential client pool within your niche to have a profitable business).

But remember, the Internet is a very large pool! The number of potential customers isn't limited by location, as it is for an offline business. Thus, you can easily have sufficient customers online, even within a very specific market.

You Don't Have to Feel "Stuck" with Your Niche Choice

After choosing your niche, you aren't immediately stuck with your choice forever—you can expand your reach later.

Once you're well established within your niche and have developed a reputation, you can expand more easily.

Here's an example: A friend of mine, Veronica, is interested in creating swimwear for women. Since there are already many established brands in the industry, she could choose to cater to a specific market, such as women with a very small breast size. She could create swimsuits specifically designed for their shape to make that "niche" of customers look their best and feel more confident. Eventually, once she's well established in her market, she could decide to expand and target women with a very large breast size, for example, and create a completely different line of swimsuits perfectly designed for the needs of *that* target clientele. Veronica could keep expanding her product lines this way by focusing on being great at serving one segment (niche) at a time.

Why Should You Choose a Niche Instead of a Broader Market?

1) You'll have a better chance of standing out and getting noticed, and you will gain authority in your field faster.

In her book *Stand Out*, Dorie Clark questions:

"In a noisy world, where it seems everything's been said—and shouted from the rooftops—how can your ideas stand out?"

She answers that operating in a niche gives an entrepreneur a better chance of being noticed and being seen as an authoritative figure or thought leader in a given field. Being a thought leader means being recognized as a knowledgeable person to seek out for specific information. Once you have become that person, you don't need to shout from the rooftops, since people will naturally come to you.

It's difficult to enter a market and compete against leaders who are already well known for their work in a given field. However, if you focus on *one* specific aspect or niche and really explore it, there is a good chance that you'll become more knowledgeable than most people and will be considered the go-to person in that specific market.

Let's return to Veronica and the swimsuit example. By choosing to serve a specific market (women with very small breasts) first, Veronica could build her brand and make a name for herself in the industry faster than if she tried to serve all types of clientele, which would mean competing against the major brands.

By not trying to serve everyone and instead focusing on specific clientele, she could differentiate herself from the other players and stand out more easily. The main idea here is that **it's easier to become a big fish in a small pond.**

2) You'll Be Making More Money

As Pat Flynn (*SmartPassiveIncome.com*) often says: *"The riches are in the niches."*

You'll make more sales.

People are looking for a specific answer to a specific problem, so they prefer to buy something that corresponds to their precise needs. They buy the "best match" possible, because they believe it will help them solve their problem the best. If you've addressed your marketing message to a specific group of people, they are more likely to feel engaged and feel that their needs are understood, and ultimately buy what you are selling.

You'll be able to sell your product or service at a higher price.

If your product is *exactly* what someone is looking for, he or she will be willing to pay more for it.

Mara Tyler is a copywriting expert. She helps website owners perfect their message in their writing. On her website, she mentions that she mainly works with coaches and people operating in fields related to health and personal development. These are the clients she prefers and has the most experience working with.

If you were a personal coach and needed help with the copywriting of your website, would you go to Mara Tyler, or to another copywriter who works with any kind of business willing to hire her? I'm sure you would pick Mara. Furthermore, since she would correspond better to your specific needs, you'll feel more confident about her capacity to solve your problem, and you will probably be willing to pay a higher fee for her services.

3) You'll Enjoy Your Work More

Marianne Cantwell from *Free-Range-Humans.com* puts it this way: "You get to *choose* your niche."

By picking a niche, you get to choose the people who you'll work with and eliminate the ones you would prefer to avoid. In short, you'll be happier. In Marianne Cantwell's opinion, choosing a niche is absolutely essential to success.

4) You'll Handle Your Marketing More Easily

Reaching a mass market (everyone) is hard! This broad-spectrum targeting is usually done through TV and newspaper advertising, which are costly and not necessarily effective.

Seth Godin, a marketing expert, says in his book, *The Purple Cow,* that there is no more room in the mass market... it's saturated! This means that trying to sell to everyone is going to be very hard work.

Targeting a mass market will put you in direct competition with the bigger players (larger companies), all of which have more capital to spend on marketing research and advertising than you do. Therefore, it's generally better to leave the mass market to the larger players.

Also, when you select a specific type of people (niche) to offer a product or a service, it's easier and faster to find where these people "hang out" (both online and offline) and find effective ways to reach them.

For example, different groups of people with distinctive objectives will use different social media platforms. Depending on the psychographic and demographic features of your market, you'll be able to determine which platform your target market uses the most. These are the platforms where you should expose your brand.

Many marketing sites, such as *Pew Research Center*, publish studies on social media users that you can use to determine where you'll have a better chance of reaching your audience.

Your topic will also determine which platform to favor. If your product is very visual, like photography, paintings, or crafts, platforms like *Instagram* and *Pinterest* work very well to transmit your message and connect with your audience.

We'll go deeper into how to reach your target market in Chapter 8, which focuses on driving traffic to your website. The main idea is that once you *know* the people who constitute your niche and know where to find them, you'll spend less time and money to reach them.

How to Choose a Niche

There are three main aspects to keep in mind when selecting a niche:

1) Choose a niche you are interested in serving.

As mentioned before, according to Marianne Cantwell (*Free-Range-Humans.com*), you have to pick the people you are interested in helping and have an affinity with. Basically, you choose the people you want to work with, because that's what will make you happy.

2) Make sure it's profitable.

You also need to make sure that your niche is profitable by answering these questions:

Do your customers have money to pay for your product or service?

For example, a single parent on social benefits probably won't have the money to buy expensive unessential goods.

Are your customers willing to spend money on your product or service?

Even people with a high salary might not hire you to take care of watering their indoor plants. They probably don't care enough. Or your offer might just not appeal to a large enough group of people to ensure that your business will be a profitable one.

Are there enough potential buyers for your business to be profitable?

How do you know if there are enough potential buyers? The easiest way when you are just starting out is by looking at the competition. Are there successful businesses already serving the same market? If so, that means there are enough buyers. Competition is usually a good sign.

3) Choose to serve the people you know.

Jeremy and Jason from *Internet Business Mastery* say that you should choose a niche that you know, since you'll need to be able to put yourself in your audience's shoes and empathize with them. You need empathy to connect with your potential customers to build trust with them and be able to sell them your product or service.

Your target audience should therefore be a past or a present version of yourself, or at least people who you understand very well, have a deep interest in serving, and can easily have access to so you can gather helpful information about their needs and desires.

However, it's important to mention that you should always do research to validate what you *think* you know about your niche. Even if your audience is a past or a present version of yourself and represents the people you think you know well, always do your research to confirm and back up what you *think* with real data, because you could be wrong.

In this information era, there is no need to guess. Today, with the Internet, you have the capacity to research and find real data. A rookie mistake is to make assumptions.

How Can You Make Sure a Niche Will Be Profitable?

1) Find paying customers.

Ramit Sethi says that before plunging full speed into your business idea, start by finding three paying customers for your product or service. If you can find three paying customers (besides your mom, dad, and best friend), then you might have a potentially profitable niche. Ramit mentions that many of his students are resistant to the idea and claim that it's a difficult thing to do. However, his answer is right: "If you can't find just three paying customers now, how can you expect to get numerous customers later?"

2) Look at the competition.

As mentioned before, if there are existing competitors in your niche who have built profitable businesses, it's proof that there are potential buyers for your offer. A complete lack of competition usually isn't a good sign.

3) Find magazines and nonfiction books related to the topic.

Are there magazines related to your niche and topic? If yes, that's also a good sign. Since it costs money to create and print magazines, there must be enough readers to justify the production cost.

4) Look for other digital products.

Are there similar products targeting the same audience that are selling well? You can find out by searching on sites like ClickBank.com or Amazon.com. If there are existing products selling well, that's good news!

5) Is there an important problem to be solved?

Your product or service should solve a "problem," which we refer to as "pain," experienced by your target market. Sometimes, the "pain" is obvious, whereas at other times, it's more difficult to identify. If you can spot a real source of pain experienced by a market and have the ability to provide a solution, then your chances of succeeding will be much higher. Note that a pain can also be an unsatisfied desire.

6) Conduct research.

You can research popular topics and business trends on these websites:

- *Magazines.com, Ezinearticles.com*
  Look at the categories and the subcategories. You can even search by best sellers to find out what's popular.
- *Amazon.com*
  Scroll through the categories and subcategories in the eBook section. Look at the bestsellers in the nonfiction results.
- *Clickbank.com*
  When you click on a category, you'll find a list of subcategories below the filter and refined search options. You can use various filters, such as the "gravity" option, to determine the popularity and performance of a particular product.
- *FindaForum.net*
  Look at the category section. If there is a forum about a topic, then it is likely an interesting market. Plus, visiting a forum is one of the best ways to get insight into the needs of a market.

Still Don't Think a Niche Is the Best Approach in Your Particular Case?

If for some reason you still don't see the need for or advantage of targeting a narrower market to sell your products, or if you have a portfolio of products that you want to sell to different types of people, remember that, at the very least, your message itself must be formulated differently for different target markets.

You have to address distinctive groups of people in a different manner. Your message must be crafted in the language (wording and expressions) used by those you are trying to reach to ensure their understanding of your offer. That's why some research is required before creating your message.

Also, once again, you should use the appropriate channels to deliver your message for each niche market where your product is being sold, depending on where your customers "hang out."

Many niches = Many messages = Many channels.

Is There a Downside in Choosing a Niche Versus a Broader Market?

Hmm... Well, yes and no.

Marianne Cantwell (*Free-Range-Human.com*) explains the balance very well. She says that choosing a niche means appealing to a specific type of people. It also means *not* appealing to all the rest. Some people will love you and will buy everything you have to offer, but inevitably, others will simply dislike your product or see no need for it. *That's* the downside.

Being "Beige" Will Attract Indifference

To have a profitable business, what you really need are 1,000 true fans. That's an idea first introduced by Kevin Kelly, in an article[2] he published a few years ago. If you have 1,000 true fans that buy everything you sell, you can generate enough revenue to make a living. But how do you make 1,000 people love you that much?

First, you differentiate yourself. Embrace your uniqueness and be true to yourself, and the *right people* will connect with you and your product or service. If you try to be appealing to as many people as possible, your offer will be bland and diluted, because everyone doesn't have the same tastes and needs.

These people might perceive your offer as "okay," but would probably not become raving fans. As said by the founders of *Fizzle.co*: *"Talking to everybody will attract you indifference."* When you address your message to everyone, no one connects with it, because no one feels particularly engaged.

Here's an example with blogging:

Ben, a member of one of my previous mastermind groups, was starting out in the fitness industry. He built a website to eventually sell his own fitness programs online. He also decided to create a blog where he could engage in a conversation with his (future) audience. As he started, he realized that there was one very important element he needed to consider: *Who would be his audience?*

---

[2] Article *1000 True Fans*, by Kevin Kelly http://kk.org/thetechnium/1000-true-fans/

If he was to write blog articles about "losing weight after pregnancy," "building muscles for men," and "exercising to reduce cholesterol," his audience would be everyone interested in fitness, for one reason or another.

If that was the case, how could he expect to engage in a meaningful conversation with so many different individuals—with different pains, needs, and motivations—all at once?

By trying to reach everyone, Ben would have probably ended up connecting with no one. Of course, he could eventually tackle all of these topics once he created a name for himself in the industry. However, he would probably attract more attention to his blog by addressing his message to a *more specific* group of people as a starting point.

What About Dealing with Criticism?

Are you scared that people won't like you, your ideas, or your product? Or worse, that they will tell you and the rest of the world how they feel? Yes, this thought is even scarier when you've put yourself and your uniqueness out there in a vulnerable way. Know that almost everyone experiences the same fear, but what do you prefer—being "beige" and bland, or standing out and taking the chance of being criticized by a few?

It's essential to take criticism with a growth mindset, meaning that you should see every challenge as an opportunity to grow.

Having a growth mindset means using all *constructive* criticism as feedback, and regarding it as an opportunity to learn and improve. Notice that I said *constructive* criticism. That's the only negative feedback you should bother to listen to and be concerned about. Unhelpful comments with the sole intention of hurting shouldn't get even a slight bit of your attention—they aren't worth it.

What to Remember about Niche Markets

1) A niche market is more specific than a mass market. When you choose to serve a niche, you choose to address your product or service to a group of people who share some demographic and/or psychographic characteristics, as well as the same goals or motivation.

2) Choosing a niche versus a mass market will make your life easier.
- You'll stand out and get noticed more easily.
- You'll be seen as a figure of authority in your field, and you will gain credibility faster.
- You can charge a higher fee for your services.

3) When choosing a niche, you should pick one that you're interested in and that you already know well. A good choice for a niche is an audience or group representing a past or present version of yourself.

4) You should also verify that this particular market will be profitable:
- Do the members have the money to pay?
- Would they be willing to pay?
- Are there enough members?

5) Don't simply make assumptions; always validate what you think through research. Guessing is a rookie mistake that could prevent you from succeeding.

6) The downside of choosing to serve a niche is that even though you will thrill some individuals (your niche), others might completely dislike or be indifferent to what you do. Take constructive criticism as an opportunity to improve, but don't concern yourself with unhelpful negative comments.

Take Action

(Suggested time to allow for the exercise: 1.5 hours)

1) Find "your people."

- What subcultures do you belong to?
- What groups of people do you identify with and feel connected to?
- Are you an intellectual?
- Do you feel very concerned about the environment?
- Are you a heavy metal music fan?
- Are you a lover of the outdoors? Etc.

2) Find out if a niche could be profitable.

Determine if your market segment (niche) could be profitable by answering these three questions:

- Do the members **have the money** to pay?
- Would they be **willing to pay**?
- Are there **enough members**?

CHAPTER 4

CONNECTING WITH YOUR AUDIENCE

Create Your Ideal Customer's Avatar Profile

Before trying to sell anything, or even before creating a product or service, you should define your audience's profile. We call this process "creating your customer's avatar," or your buyer persona's profile.

Andrew Lock (*HelpMyBusiness.com*) explains this concept very well:

"Your avatar—or buyer persona, if you prefer—is a fictional representation of your ideal customer based on real data."

Why Should You Bother Creating an Avatar?

Because you are *not* your customer.

You may be a past or even a current version of your target audience, but consider this—just the mere fact that you are creating a product distinguishes you from your customers. You are not *exactly* like them.

Therefore, to be able to determine what *they* would find valuable enough to give you their money for, you first need to know them well, because you'll need to think from their perspective. The best way to do this is by creating the most realistic version of one, two, or even three different members of your ideal audience. And yes, to create such a profile, you should use real data.

This process should be taken very seriously, because it can have a tremendous impact on the overall success of your business. The founders of *Fizzle.co* clearly state this in their entrepreneurial program:

"You can give your business a much better chance of success by investing time up front getting to know the audience, understanding their problems, their language, and their values so the chances of creating a successful business for that audience are much higher. The key is: get the right head, heart, and data about your audience and make something valuable for them!"

How to Create Your *Ideal* Customer's Avatar Profile

First, I'd like to point out the emphasis on the term *ideal*.

We want you to work with customers who are interesting to you and exclude the others. That's why we'll create those *ideal* customers' profiles—these are the customers you'll try to reach.

So what should these profiles contain?

- o   Demographic Description:
    - Age
    - Gender
    - Location: Where do they live?
    - Occupation: What kind of work do they do? Do they work full time or part time? Are they students?
    - Income
    - Marital status and family situation: Are they married? Single? Do they have kids?

- o   Psychographic Description:
    - Lifestyle
    - Values
    - Priorities
    - Hobbies: How do they spend their free time?
    - Behavior and attitude
    - What do they care about?
    - What are their dreams?
    - What's their definition of success?

- o   Goals and Motivation:
    What drives them? For example, a woman who wants to lose post-pregnancy weight and a man who wants to build muscles don't share to same motivation to hit the gym.

- o   "Pain":
    - Struggles
    - Fears
    - Concerns
    - What is missing in their lives?

The more information you can gather, the better. Knowing your ideal customers will make it easier for you to find out where they "hang out." Once you know where to find them (on which social media platform, for example), you'll be able to listen to the conversations they are having.

You'll learn to speak your customers' language, and you will be able to communicate with them more effectively. You'll detect and understand their problems, goals, and motivations, and then be better suited to create the best solution (product) for them.

That's how you'll make more sales. Obviously, the customers' avatars that you will create won't represent *all* members of your audience perfectly, but you should be aware of and look for commonalities among the members of your niche.

Here's an example of a customer profile for a business that offers an online video course:

Name: Joshua

Age: Between 25 and 35 years old.

Lives in New Jersey, in an apartment, alone.

Single, no children.

Works as a programmer in a small firm.

Income: 60,000 - 70,000/year.

He drives to work.

He works Monday to Friday, from 8am to 6pm, and has the weekends off. His current job bores him, and he feels his life is lacking excitement. He would like to make a career change and maybe even work as a freelancer to have more flexibility with his schedule.

A short time ago, he chose to actively change his situation. He decided to go on a two-month trip to South America by himself—something he has never done before. He hopes that this time away will allow him to make a decision about the direction of his career. He bought a camera to make a video of his trip. Before he leaves, he hopes to learn how to use the camera and make videos. He is currently looking for a course that can teach him the basics of filming and editing. He wants to know how to use his camera properly within a short period of time before going on the trip three months from now.

This brief story gives an idea of a buyer persona for a company offering online photography and video classes. The profile could be even more detailed and include other potentially useful information about his goals and motivations.

Note: When defining your buyers' personas, be careful not to make this mistake.

If you wanted to offer singing lessons to children under the age of 12, who would your target audience be? Did you say "children under 12"? Intuitively, that's what most people would answer, but think about it... How could a seven-year-old buy singing lessons? Seven-year-olds don't have disposable incomes. The target audience would be the child's parents – the ones who would make the purchase – making them the people to whom the message must be addressed.

Where Do You Find Information About Your Ideal Customer?

Do you remember when we mentioned the word *data*? Of course, you may intuitively have an idea regarding what your ideal customer looks like, but one rule to remember is to *never assume.* You'll have to do some research.

The research will differ if you already have an audience (past or current customers, clients, or blog readers) versus if you are starting from scratch. However, even if you don't have an existing audience, you can find valuable information online and offline after just a few hours of research.

Here are some tactics you can use:

1) Interview someone you know.

Your task is easier when you know a person who represents your target market.

You can already define some demographic traits, and even several psychographic ones, like the person's lifestyle or hobbies. Then, all you have to do is to invite that person out for a coffee and ask him or her questions about their goals, motivations, struggles, fears and desires. If you know two or three people, that's even better! Interview them all, but do it separately.

2) Meet new people.

Meet new people who represent your target market.

Where? Meetup groups, for example, are a great way. *Meetup.com* is a platform that facilitates connections between people who share the same interests. On their website, you simply select your city and search for groups related to your business topic. These groups organize meetings and events in person—and sometimes online—that allow their members to connect with like-minded people. You can join a group related to your niche or even create a new one.

I have personally created a Meetup group to exchange ideas about Internet marketing, online business and blogging. In the beginning, I thought the group would help me progress faster in creating my projects by holding me accountable. However, it ended up being more valuable for writing this book! Hearing members talk about the progress of their own businesses gave me great insights about the struggles around web marketing for new entrepreneurs and freelancers. It helped me discern the most relevant concepts to write about.

3) Ask people who work or deal with your target market.

For example, if you wanted to offer online Spanish classes, you could ask a college Spanish teacher to share his or her observations about students' motivations and difficulties in learning the language.

4) Visit the forums.

Go to FindAForum.net and search for one related to your niche.

When you select a forum, you'll see the most popular keywords people have used and a list of topics covered. Browse the threads (conversation topics). You'll have an idea of the most popular topics by the number of views, comments and replies.

Then, read the conversations. You'll learn about your niche's problems, struggles, questions, etc. Sometimes, you can also find information about the members, such as their gender, age, and location, through their profile description.

You should also observe what language they use, including the expressions, wording, and slang. As we'll discuss in more detail later, using your audience's language is very important to build a connection and trust and to eventually convert members into customers.

When you craft your message—in emails, on your website's About page, in your blog posts, in your advertising campaigns—you should use the same language.

5) Join Yahoo groups, Facebook groups and LinkedIn groups.

Join groups related to your niche and go through the same process you used with the forums. You can easily get an idea of the demographic traits of the members on Facebook and LinkedIn. Once again, observe the conversations. You could also easily take part in the conversations and ask questions within the groups.

6) Find popular blogs in your niche.

Find influential blogs in your niche. Search for the most popular posts published to get an idea of the popular topics. Then, look at the comments left by readers at the end of the posts. Again, note the language used by the audience, and try to find the "struggles" or the concerns that are expressed or suggested in the comments.

7) Use surveys to ask questions.

Even if you don't already have an audience, you could survey people representing your niche market, depending on the context. The survey should be short. Think of the most useful information you'd like to obtain.

If your target audience members are students, you could ask a teacher to survey them during a class. If your audience is "yoga beginners," you could ask a local yoga center to help you collect data and offer to give them the compiled results. In some contexts, it will be more difficult to gather information this way, but it is sometimes possible.

You could also use social media platforms. For example, Facebook groups have a tab that allows you to survey the group members.

8) Visit *Quora.com*.

Quora.com is a website where anyone can ask a question about anything, and experts (or anyone who has an answer) can respond. By looking for popular questions in your topic, you can identify concerns, struggles, and questions that people have. You'll know if a question on Quora is popular by the number of upvotes—this tells you that several people were interested in knowing the answer. You can also ask a question yourself and see if it gets upvoted.

9) Listen to podcasts.

You could search for podcasts related to your topic in the iTunes Store. Podcast episodes in the form of "questions and answers" are particularly valuable for your research, since you'll get an idea of questions that people in your market have asked.

Also, the podcast host has almost certainly done his or her own research to choose topics relevant to his or her audience, so podcasts can give you an idea of which topics you should explore.

Many of the above suggestions were for web businesses that were just starting out, but if you already have an audience, there's even more you can do:

10) Survey your audience via your email list or your Facebook fan page (or Facebook group).

If you have a blog or a website and have collected emails through a subscription tool, you can survey your audience by sending them an email. It's very simple and highly effective.

You could also ask a question in the "thank you" email that is automatically sent to new subscribers to your email list. This way, you can continuously get insight about your audience's current situation.

Maybe you won't ask them questions about their income or marital status, but you could survey them about what they need the most help with. You can also ask these questions in a Facebook post and invite your Facebook fans to respond in the comments below.

11) Look at comments on your own blog or Facebook page.

Read the comments that your readers, clients, or customers have left. Look for attitudes, patterns, reactions, etc.

12) Look at data on Facebook Insights and Google Analytics.

When you create a Facebook business page, you have access to data regarding your page's visitors, like basic demographics—origin, gender, and age group—through the "Insights" tab. You can also see which posts have had the most engagement (clicks, shares, and comments).

Once your website is created, you should set up an account with Google Analytics (Google.com/analytics). It's a free tool from Google that gives you data about the origin and other demographics of the visitors to your website and the sources of traffic.

Why All This Effort?

Because one of the most important aspects of marketing is *empathy*.

Wait... empathy? What does empathy have to do with all this?

Well, everything!

You gain customers, clients, or readers once you have been able *to put yourself in their shoes* and *speak their language*. You make sales *after* you have built connections and trust. That's exactly what empathy will help you do.

Once you have defined your ideal customers' profiles, you should take a few minutes to create an empathy map.

Simply write, in about half a page, what the average day of those avatars looks like from the moment they wake up to the moment they go back to bed. Do they wake up with an alarm clock? Do they drive to work through heavy traffic? Where do they work? How is their relationship with their colleagues? What do they think, feel, and say? What are they concerned or excited about? Do they play sports, or watch TV? Put yourself in your avatars' shoes and experience a day in their lives for the length of one written paragraph. That's called empathy mapping.

Why Is All of This Important?

In *80/20 Sales and Marketing,* Perry Marshall writes:

"One of the cardinal rules of marketing is to never go into a market unless you can write a page of your customers' diary and be so spooky-accurate that they wonder: 'Hey, were you spying on me last night?' That way, you won't make the mistake of jumping into a

swimming pool that has no water in it. Don't try to sell something that nobody wants to buy."

Does that help you understand the importance of empathy? While planning to create products or services for your market, you absolutely need to put yourself in your customers' shoes and see life from their perspective in order to accurately create solutions they will want to buy.

That's the main reason you have spent so much effort defining your niche market and why you have chosen one that you know and/or have a deep interest in serving. It's also why you've spent time defining the profile (avatar) of this niche. Is this all starting to make sense?

Knowing your audience—and its daily reality—is crucial for every aspect of your business. It will reflect in the copy of your website, primarily in the About page, homepage, blog posts, and sales pages.

It's also what will make your email marketing efficient, as we'll see in Chapter 7. Although they say that an email list is an organization's most important asset, it's actually the relationship that you nurture with the subscribers to your list that is even more valuable. In order to build those strong relationships, you need to demonstrate empathy. Then, and only then, will the subscribers like you, trust you, and buy from you.

What to Remember About Your Ideal Customer

1) Your ideal customers' avatar, or buyer persona, is a fictional representation of your ideal customers' profiles based on real data.

2) Expert marketers know the importance of defining their ideal customers accurately and with precision. That way, they can detect and understand their customers' problems and create products or services that will best solve them.

3) The product creation phase comes *after* you understand your audience.

4) There are many ways you can find information to help you create your customers' avatar profiles. With Internet access, you can go through this process within a few hours.

5) Good marketing is done by being able to put yourself in your customers' shoes and see life from their perspective. This is called "empathy."

Take Action

(Suggested time to allow for the exercise: 4 hours)

Take an afternoon, or even a day, to research and define your ideal customer profile.

1) Create two or three different avatars for your target customers.

Include demographic and psychographic traits. Mention what their goals and motivations are.

2) Learn their language.

Create a document in which you note the wording, expressions, and slang that they use. You'll use the same terms when addressing them.

3) Search for their "pain."

Find out what they struggle with, what problems they have, what frustrations they live with, etc.

4) Put yourself in their shoes.

See life from their perspective and think of solutions to their current situation. How could you best improve their lives? What value could you bring that they would be willing to give you money for?

5) Create an empathy map.

Describe a day in the life of your customer's avatar.

CHAPTER 5

DEFINING YOUR BRAND

What's Branding?

Essentially, your brand is your identity.

Your brand represents how you want the world to see you, and it's also how the world does see you. In fact, good branding is located at the intersection of these two perspectives, and brand management works to keep a company in that zone.

Your identity is a mixture of tangible and intangible elements, which, altogether, contribute to creating a mental image of your organization in consumers' minds. It is your job to make sure the world sees the real you, and that this mental representation of your organization is close to the image you want to project.

Your brand should differentiate you from other players in your field – your competitors – and it will also determine who your buyers will be. Some consumers will choose you over other options on the market because of your remarkable offer and because they have connected with your brand, most likely on an emotional level.

In this chapter, we'll explain the different aspects that make up your brand. You'll have to answer basic questions, such as:

- What do you do?
- Why do you do it?
- Who is your business directed towards?
- How do you do it?

Your Essence

The intangible components of your brand are crucial. These are the essence of your identity. They are the reason that potential customers will connect with your organization, buy your product or service, stay loyal, and, hopefully, become ambassadors of your brand. You can define your "essence" by answering these questions:

What do you do?

This first question is quite straightforward. What do you offer to the market? What type of product or service do you create and/or sell? What is your blog or your book about? What are you teaching at your conferences or in your courses?

How do you do it?

What are the characteristics of your offer? What materials do you use? How do you promote and deliver your offer?

We'll get into more details about this aspect later, in the section about differentiation and the unique selling proposition.

Who is your business directed towards?

Who's your target market? If you've read the chapters about niche markets and your audience profile, then you've already determined who your ideal customer is.

Why do you do it?

What's your purpose?

In his book, *Start with Why,* Simon Sinek demonstrates that great organizations are those built on a strong purpose. He states that "people don't buy what you do, they buy 'why' you do it."

At a TedX Conference, he presented Apple (the company) as an example of how organizations should operate to truly connect with their target market and sell more of their products.

Apple doesn't just make great computers, according to Sinek; that would be a pretty ordinary marketing message. "Apple believes in challenging the status quo, and in thinking differently. They create beautifully designed and simple to use computers."

Furthermore, they create computers for a specific target market – the market that shares its values and beliefs. That's the purpose of Apple, the "why" behind what it creates, which builds such a strong connection with its target consumers.

Why do you do what you do? Why do you wake up every morning? What drives you?

Why do you want to create a line of swimwear? A travel blog? A consulting business? A yoga course? If your only desire is to generate money, that's a poor "why." A real purpose is more profound than simply generating an income. Of course, the reason behind every business is to generate a profit, but the purpose behind why you started the business itself goes far beyond that.

Your Values, and What You Stand For

What do you stand for and support?

Perhaps your political beliefs are very important to you. Maybe you are environmentally conscious, or buy fair trade products, or only eat organic food. Maybe you stand for the right to education for every child around the world, or are very sensitive to gender equality. What topics are you most sensitive about?

Now, think of your core values. What adjectives would you like people to use to describe you, your company, and your product? Are you bold and adventurous, or are you disciplined and down-to-earth?

Defining your core values is an important step, not only in order to describe your organization, but also to give you a guideline to follow. It will help you decide which projects to take on, which collaborators to work with, and which future employees to hire, because all these decisions should be made in alignment with your core values.

For example, here are the core values of Zappos, a major online shoe retailer:

- Deliver WOW Through Service
- Embrace and Drive Change
- Create Fun and a Little Weirdness
- Be Adventurous, Creative, and Open-Minded
- Pursue Growth and Learning
- Build Open and Honest Relationships with Communication
- Build a Positive Team and Family Spirit
- Do More With Less
- Be Passionate and Determined
- Be Humble

Your core values become your company's culture code. They guide your decisions and determine the kind of people you'll connect and build relationships with. They also determine who will be interested in doing business with you.

Your Mission and Vision Statements

Mission

Now that you have thoroughly thought about the what, how, and why of your business, summarize it in your mission statement.

Your mission statement is a one- or two-sentence explanation of what your business is about and its reason for existing. Your mission statement should be inspirational. As Richard Branson, founder of the Virgin Group, says:

"Brevity is certainly key, so try using Twitter's 140-character template when you're drafting your inspirational message. You need to explain your company's purpose and outline expectations for internal and external clients alike. Make it unique to your company, make it memorable, and keep it real."

A mission statement should be general enough to stay relevant for several years, but still contain enough information to understand the core purpose, personality, and offerings of a company. It should become a fundamental guide for your daily actions. This information is usually found in the About section of a company's website.

Here are examples:

Hubspot.com (Online marketing company)

"To make the world Inbound. We want to transform how organizations attract, engage, and delight their customers."

Amazon.com

"To be Earth's most customer-centric company where people can find and discover anything they want to buy online."

As another example, this could be the mission statement for a **swimwear designer**:

"We believe all women should feel beautiful, so we design original swimwear that makes them feel glamorous and comfortable in their own skin."

Vision

Your vision is the roadmap for your business's future. Where do you see your business in one year? In three years? In five years?

Your vision is like the larger goal or dream behind your business — the optimal desired future state. Through your vision, you should express your ideals and what you wish to accomplish on a larger scale than just within your organization.

The bottom line is that who you are in business should be a reflection of who you are in your personal life. Defining your values, purpose, and what you stand for, as well as remaining true to them, will inspire trust and respect from your audience.

You Versus Others (Differentiation)

"When you are one of a kind, there is no competition." —Sam Horn, author of *Pop!: Create the Perfect Pitch, Title, and Tagline for Anything*

Be Different, Not Better

As Sally Hogshead, author of the book *Fascinate*, states:

"Different is better than better."

It's hard to become the best player in a given field, because the title of "best" is subjective and difficult to evaluate. Furthermore, engaging in such a competitive approach is like getting into a rat race—there will always be other players trying to beat you at your own game. This kind of endless race is energy-consuming, and unless you have unlimited marketing and advertising funds, it's not a viable approach.

Therefore, it would be smarter and more effective to capitalize on something else: your uniqueness.

No one has the exact same background and experience as yours. The combination of your story, values, mission, perspective, and what you stand for is unique. This is the one place where you are sure to win; no one can beat you at being yourself.

Maybe this sounds a little cheesy, but I believe it should also be a relief to know that all you have to do is take some time to be introspective and answer a few questions about yourself, and about what you want to share with the world to correctly define your identity—your brand.

Tell Your Story

A great way to differentiate your brand is through a story—your story! Think of a fun anecdote about the creation of your business, or about the Aha! moment when you first stumbled upon the idea.

Talk about that evening at the park when you and your best friend chatted about how easy it would be to do _____ if only _____ existed.

Michael Port, author of *Book Yourself Solid* and *Steal The Show*, suggests that people create a library of their stories.

These stories can be related to important people, places, events or things in our lives. For example, a first date, a memorable vacation or a childhood family home might all fit within this collection. If you think of the first time you went on a plane, a story might come to mind. The same is true for the first time you invited someone on a date, etc. Port suggests writing down and collecting those stories, and to eventually use them by creating analogies to illustrate ideas.

Stories are a great way to develop a connection. They humanize your business and allow people to bond with you and your ideas more easily. They raise the connection with your audience to an emotional level.

Your Unique Selling Proposition

Your unique selling proposition (USP) is how you do what you do in a way that is different from the other players in your field. It's how you differentiate yourself from your competitors. It's your unique, competitive advantage—the benefit only *you* can offer.

Basically, your USP should be formulated in a very clear message that explains your offer (product or service), and why it should be chosen over the other options available on the market. To achieve this, the proposition must be remarkable and must promise outstanding value.

I personally believe that it is quite difficult to offer one completely unique advantage, especially if the advantage is being "the best at something"—like offering the lowest price, the highest quality, or the best customer service. Some organizations do use this kind of USP, but by doing so, they enter the same rat race we mentioned earlier. I have found that a viable unique selling proposition should be a combination of elements that, when brought together, make your offer original and irresistible.

If we take the example of the swimwear designer again, a unique selling proposition could be:

"We create great quality swimwear pieces for women that are entirely unique—there are no two pieces in the same size for each design—that fit their body type perfectly and make them feel beautiful and comfortable in their own skin. All our swimwear is made locally with environmentally-friendly methods and materials."

There are many swimwear designers, but not all of them offer this same value:

- Unique pieces
- Great body fit
- Made locally
- Made using environmentally-friendly methods and materials

To determine your USP, it helps to think of the "problem" in your niche that you are trying to solve and of the method you'll use to do so. If you have identified a "pain" in your niche that hasn't been tackled, or at least not in the same way as you do, then you already have an idea of your USP. Your unique approach to solving the problem, if it's not easy to imitate, is a competitive advantage.

Simply by having chosen to serve a niche versus a broader market will make it easier for you to come up with a strong USP. Business coach Mark McGuiness (LateralAction.com) specializes in coaching artists, such as actors, writers, and musicians. His unique selling proposition clearly states that his expertise is directed towards helping individuals operating in creative fields to build their creative business or take it to the next level. Being a creative (poet) himself, he can better serve his target market. For an entrepreneur in a creative field, this is far more interesting than hiring a more general coach.

It can also help if your product is more specific. For example, a graffiti artist could choose to specialize in painting natural objects, such as trees, plants, and mountains, in very industrial and gloomy neighborhoods to enliven them. That artist would stand out from other graffiti artists.

Before finishing up with differentiation, I would like to illustrate how we sometimes tend to do it wrong, with a personal example. When I created my first blog on healthy lifestyle, I tried to copy the bigger sites like Mind Body Green, Tiny Buddha, and even Inc.com. I thought my site should look like theirs to appear professional and credible, and to become popular. I spent hours installing the same plugins they used and designing my site to look somewhat similar to theirs.

Do you see how wrong I was? I shot myself in the foot—in both feet, actually!—trying to look like the big players. What chance did I have of competing against industry leaders who were already ranked very high in Google, got tons of page views per day and had a huge social media following? I placed my website side-by-side with the more popular sites with NO differentiation. Not a wise move.

It's not smart to compete on the same stage as the big players, especially not when you're just starting out and have zero audience, credibility, and authority. The only way you can get noticed is by not doing the same thing as everyone else!

Positioning

Positioning your product well is just as important as the product itself. It determines how it will be received by the market, and therefore determines its success. Your goal should be to get the right people to purchase your product, rather than just selling as many of your products as possible.

This is extremely important, because you don't want to gain numerous unhappy customers who could become anti-ambassadors for your brand.

The Business Dictionary defines positioning as:

"An effort to influence consumer perception of a brand or product relative to the perception of competing brands or products. Its objective is to occupy a clear, unique, and advantageous position in the consumer's mind."

Positioning is how you are compared to your competitors in consumers' minds. It's your unique selling proposition in comparison to those of other players. The difference between your USP and positioning is that positioning is based completely on the consumers' perceptions—it's the image of your organization or product from their perspective.

Maybe you won't perform comprehensive market research to learn about the perception towards your brand versus your competitors, but some elements will automatically categorize you within the market.

Pricing is one fundamental element. Will you be a low-cost, average, or high-end option? Pricing has a very psychological effect. A higher price is usually associated with higher quality, and is seen as more exclusive. The price of your offer will also determine the type of clientele you'll work with. Therefore, pricing, as a component of positioning (and branding), should be aligned with the niche market you have chosen to serve. Other elements of positioning include the product itself, the communication surrounding its promotion, and the way it's delivered to the market.

To illustrate how the wrong positioning can lead to a product's failure, think of an online course for learning Spanish. If the course is designed at an intermediate level and focuses on Latin American Spanish, this should be explicitly mentioned in the course description.

Why? Because a true beginner learning the language and planning a trip to Spain might be disappointed by what the course delivers. The language is slightly different in Spain than in Latin America, plus the learner might have trouble understanding the lessons because the course is taught at an intermediate level. The product would simply not be appropriate for this learner's needs.

Before defining the position you would like to acquire in the market, take a look at your competitors and at what has already been done. This will help you to have a better idea of where to position your brand.

The Tangible Elements That Support Your Essence

Your Organization and Product or Service Name

The name of your organization does matter. It should be simple to understand, to spell, to remember, and to associate with your offer.

Ideally, it should easily create a mental image of what you are all about in your consumers' minds... the right image.

The same is true for your product or service names.

Your Visual Identity

You need to choose your visual identity carefully, because it's not something you will change much over time. This visual representation of your brand has to be consistent on all platforms, in social media, and in other promotional material.

Colors and Fonts

In branding, consistency is a basic rule to respect. You don't want to create confusion in your consumer's mind. You want to build a strong brand, and visual elements are a crucial component of the image associated with your organization. This means that the colors and fonts you decide to use to create your visual identity should be consistent.

Certain colors evoke certain emotions and perceptions, and are associated with certain types of businesses and fields. For example, if you offer gardening services, it would be natural to choose green tones, but not as many purple tones. In fact, purple is often associated with alternative medicines. Blue is a color of trust and professionalism, whereas orange often relates to creativity.

Depending on the type of business you have, the field you operate in, and how you want people to perceive you, you'll choose a certain color palette to support your branding efforts.

Do some research about the meaning of colors to make sure that they are aligned with your offer, purpose, and values. Visit sites like ColourLovers.com, which provide color palettes created by designers. The website also shows trends and even the color palettes used by known brands (avoid picking the same colors as your competitors!).

The fonts you use should also reinforce the identity of your business. For example, a law firm wouldn't look very professional using a typographical script style on its website.

Logo

As with a name, a logo must be simple and easily recognizable. It shouldn't look similar to someone else's, as it's an important element used to differentiate yourself from other players.

Your logo is an important part of your branding. It will appear on your promotional material, on your business cards, on your website, in your email signature, etc. It's like a signature in itself.

Choosing a logo isn't easy. That's why you should ideally delegate the task to an expert—a graphic designer. The more information you can give the designer about your company, the more likely you'll be to get a logo that represents your organization well.

You can hire a designer to create your logo though a freelancing platform like UpWork.com or DesignHill.com. Contest-based services are another option, like 99 designs.com, where you pay a fixed price and get several offers, from which you can choose the logo you like best.

Website

Don't try to make your website look similar to your competitors' sites, in the hopes that it will make you look more professional (remember that mistake I once made?). Aim to be different.

If you aren't a designer yourself, you could hire a professional to help you. You can hire a designer to create your whole visual identity on sites like DesignHill.com. It's something you create once, and it's definitely worth it to spend a little bit of money to have it done right.

Your Communication

Another subtler component of branding is your tone of voice.

Your tone of voice is the way you communicate your message and the language you use through different platforms and channels. It's closely related to the personality of your brand, to your core values, and to your chosen approach.

If you offer consulting services, sell online courses, or host workshops, your tone will primarily be educational. You'll use proper, respectful, and easy-to-understand language to make sure your audience clearly gets your message. If you write a travel blog and mainly tell anecdotes, maybe you'll choose a more casual or even humorous tone. You have to decide: Are you more formal or chatty? Serious or funny? Detached or warm? Opinionated or neutral?

As a brand component, your voice should be aligned with your values, mission, vision, and all the other elements that contribute to creating the correct image for your organization, which is the image you want to produce in your consumer's mind.

Determine the tone you will use in your communication based on the nature of your business and on your own personality, and be consistent. If you've chosen a neutral tone, you probably won't initiate a politically-charged conversation on social media.

Express Your Brand

Elevator Pitch

When people ask, "What do you do?" are you able to answer right away? It's not always easy.

Can you tell people, in less than 40 seconds, who you are and what you do in a way that will make them curious to know more? That's basically what an elevator pitch is: introducing who you are and what you do in a way that quickly captures your audience's interest and makes them sufficiently intrigued to want to know more about your "cause" (your idea, project, organization or product).

Ben Parr, author of *Captivology: The Science Of Capturing People's Attention*, says that there are three stages of attention:

1) Immediate attention: something in our environment that grabs our attention, at a specific moment.
2) Short attention: when we consciously give our focused attention to something that triggered our interest.
3) Long attention: something that has attracted our long-term interest.

Parr says that it is necessary to go through all the stages of attention to reach long-term interest, which is what you want. Essentially, there is no shortcut. In other words, grabbing someone's attention and attracting their conscious attention must happen before we can engage them or encourage them to remember us.

We must be careful, however, as an elevator pitch is not about showing off. People don't connect with braggarts. Every pitch is focused on inspiring interest in others about what you have to offer. It's about transmitting your passion, what you stand for, and what you are building and working on.

It also demonstrates why an idea is interesting for others, because even if your elevator pitch is obviously about you, it's also about them. Remember, in the end, it's always about them. "Don't make people wonder what it has to do with them. Make them feel concerned."—Sam Horn, author of *POP!*

Therefore, making people engaged in your "cause" is important. They will listen to you more attentively if they feel that the information concerns them. If you want to make an impact, make your pitch engaging.

Note that you will facilitate engagement if you use your audience's language. It's important to avoid jargon and expert terms; instead, communicate your message using wording that is easy to understand. Metaphors are also a great way to help people remember your brand. For example, "Our swimwear is so comfortable, it feels like a second skin."

Why does the elevator pitch have to be less than 40 seconds? Because the attention span of most people is very limited. With an average of only eight seconds, it's even shorter than the attention span of a goldfish (Microsoft study, 2015). This means that if you don't intrigue someone enough within the first 10 seconds, their mind might already be wandering elsewhere.

All that being said, here's the structure of a good elevator pitch:

1) Intrigue them (5-10 seconds)
2) Give a few details so they understand the idea better (5-10 seconds)

3) Tell them why it's important, and why they should feel concerned (5-10 seconds)
4) Let them know that there's more they should know about it (5-10 seconds)

Here's an elevator pitch example for a swimwear designer:

"We help women feel glamorous and comfortable in their own skin (**intrigue**).

We design unique pieces of swimwear for women that perfectly fit with their own body type, and enhance their features. We believe that every woman should feel beautiful. Our swimwear is elegant, and also adapted to an active lifestyle. It allows comfort and ease of movement (**give details**).

All our swimwear is made locally with environmentally-friendly methods and materials. When you buy our product, you also contribute to an environmental cause, since 10% of the profits go to a water preservation organization (**make them feel concerned**).

Our swimwear can be found online and in a few physical stores (**make them want to learn more**)."

Tagline

"A tagline is a one-sentence summary of your story. Its goal is to intrigue and make the person that you are delivering it to want to read the whole story. The most important thing about the tagline is that it needs to be high concept. It should sum up the entire plot in one quick, compelling sentence." –Stacey Nash, author

A tagline is shorter than an elevator pitch. It could be the elevator pitch's first sentence—the intriguing part, the attention grabber. It also illustrates the "big picture" of what you do.

Here are some well-known companies' taglines:

- Apple: "Think different."
- Pepsi: "The uncola."
- Avis (car rental): "We try harder."
- Barack Obama: "Change we need."
- Disneyland: "The happiest place on earth."
- L'Oréal: "Because you're worth it."

If you were walking down the street with a tag stuck on your forehead stating what your business is about in five words, what would it say?

Rules to Respect

There are three main rules to respect in branding: alignment, clarity and consistency.

Alignment

We have already mentioned how important it is to align your branding efforts. Your message (tone) should be aligned with your values and purpose. The same goes for your visual identity, which should also be chosen based on the nature of your organization and offering (product or service type). Congruence is key. It's almost impossible to inspire trust if all the elements that compose your brand aren't aligned. Your business would look "sketchy."

Clarity

It's also your job to make sure that the message you send to your target market is crystal clear so that your offer is well understood. As they say, a confused mind doesn't buy. Use simple language, not industry language that the average consumer won't understand.

Don't hide details about your offer. People get annoyed when information is missing or when they don't fully understand what's being presented.

Consistency

Remember to be consistent with the tone of your communication and in the visual aspect of your brand (colors, fonts, logo, and design). You want people to easily recognize your organization.

Brand Management

Brand Monitoring

To stay on the lookout for what's being said about your brand, tools like Google Alerts allow you to receive updates when your brand is mentioned on the Internet. You can use the same tool to monitor what's being said about your competitors.

Also, pay attention to the comments your audience makes about you on social media, in the comment section of your blog, or elsewhere.

Convergence Zone

If there's a gap between what is being said about you and how you want to be perceived, it means that you've ventured outside the "convergence zone." Good branding is about staying in the convergence zone.

If something is said about you that you don't appreciate, try to understand what triggered that comment and make the necessary adjustments in your activities or communication.

What to Remember About Branding

1) Your brand is, essentially, your business identity.

2) Your brand includes several tangible and intangible components, such as:
- Visual elements—logo, promotional material and website design, colors and fonts
- The name of your organization and of your products or services
- Your tone of voice
- Your purpose
- Your core values and what you stand for
- Your unique selling proposition
- Your position in the market

3) Your brand must be summarized in a clear and concise message that becomes your tagline and your elevator pitch.

4) Good branding is in the convergence zone of "how you want the world to see you" and "how the world actually sees you."

5) Clarity, alignment, and consistency are the three main rules to respect in branding.

Take Action

(Suggested time to allow for the exercise: 5 hours)

This process can be longer. It may take several weeks to come up with a clear brand idea, but it's worth the time and effort—it's your identity, after all!

1) Why do you do what you do? Define your purpose.

2) Develop a library of stories—personal anecdotes and other stories related to your business.

3) How do you do what you do? Define your unique selling proposition.

What are you offering that no one else is? What's different or unique about your offer that will make your audience choose you over your competitors?

4) Create your elevator pitch.

- o Explain, in about 20 to 40 seconds, what your business is about.
- o Intrigue them (5-10 seconds)
- o Give a few details so they can understand the idea better (5-10 seconds)
- o Tell them why it's important, and why they should feel concerned (5-10 seconds)
- o Let them know that there's more they should know about your business (5-10 seconds)

5) Create your tagline.

Create an intriguing, attention-grabbing short sentence (about 5 words) that illustrates what you do.

6) Make an overview of your visual identity.

What colors and font do you use? Do they represent the nature of your business well? Is it consistent?

7) Make an overview of your communication efforts.

This includes your communication on social media, on your website, and on promotional material:

- What tone of voice do you use? Is it more educational or opinionated, serious or humorous, engaged or neutral, etc.?
- Do you walk your talk? Is your voice aligned with your values?
- Is your message clear to understand?

CHAPTER 6

GETTING PAST THE TECHNICAL ASPECTS

The technical part of an online business isn't really an element of the blueprint—it's not a determinant of your success—but as it is a major concern for many aspiring online entrepreneurs, I felt that we had to explore this aspect, as well.

If you're comfortable with technology, building your website and adding plugins (pieces of software code), then this won't be difficult for you at all. However, for less tech-savvy individuals, technology can be stressful... at least until you begin to understand how it works.

We won't spend much time explaining the technical part of starting an online business, but I will direct you to some good resources that can help.

If the Internet (or even computers themselves) makes you nervous, just take a deep breath—you'll see that it's really not too complicated. I'm not a tech-savvy person, and I still manage to enjoy the technical part of my business.

Choosing a Platform

You have two main options when building your website: self-hosted or *not* self-hosted.

To be found on the Web, it is essential that your website be "hosted" on a server. Web hosting is basically a service provided by a company that enables your website to be seen online. It's a bit like the online version of renting a physical space in a shopping center, so your store can be visited by potential buyers.

Option 1) Hosted platform

You could choose to build your site on a hosted platform, such as:

- WordPress.**com** (different from WordPress.**org**)
- Weebly.com
- SquareSpace.com
- RainMakerPlatform.com (high-end option)

These platforms manage the software, data and web hosting for you—they host your website content on their own web server.

This is a simpler option, and often an appropriate one for a "display" type of website. However, as you continue building your business, the functions will be too limited for your needs in the long run. You would need better SEO capabilities and other special features to help you grow your business. Therefore, I do *not* recommend this option.

Option 2) Self-hosted

This is the option I recommend. To be more specific, I recommend using the content management system, WordPress.**org** (different from WordPress.**com**).

This option includes registering a domain name, purchasing a web hosting plan and connecting them to WordPress.org. We'll explain each step.

Choosing a Domain Name

You'll need to purchase a domain for your new website, which usually costs around $10/year.

You can register your domain through sites like OnlyDomains.com, GoDaddy.com or NameCheap.com. However, I would recommend that you purchase it directly with your web hosting provider. This will be less confusing.

What is a *good* domain name?

First, it will have to be available. With an ever-growing number of websites, many domains are already used. When you enter a domain name (on your hosting provider website), it will tell you if the domain is available or already taken. In most cases, it's better to use ".com" than any other domain endings (.org, .co, .ca).

Also, try to find a domain that doesn't use hyphens, underscores, numbers, or complicated (hard to spell) words. Make it as easy as possible for potential visitors to remember your website address and type it in the browser. You want them to be able to find you!

Another thing to consider: Try to avoid confusion with other brand names and domains. If the domain you want is taken, should you add a prefix to it, or a hyphen? For example, if you had decided on SpeedCars.com, but it's already taken, should you use Speed-cars.com, if it's available? Well, you might get easily confused with the other company, which isn't a good thing. You would also need to check if the trademark "speed cars" is registered. If it is, you could risk a legal suit by using the name.

Your domain name should also make sense for your business. Ideally, it would include your business name, or the main activity or topic of your business. For example, YogaStudio.com is obviously about yoga. Later in the book, we'll talk about the importance of keywords. Ideally, your domain would contain main keywords (terms) that describe what your business is about.

Basically, you want a domain name that is easy to remember and spell, and that makes sense for your business. Also, choose one that doesn't confuse your brand with another's, and ideally use a ".com" ending.

Web hosting service

You'll also need a web hosting service, for which you can expect to pay around $5-$10/month. It's very important to select a reliable service, and I recommend BlueHost.com or HostGator.com. They both have 99.9% uptime (time your site is running) and provide excellent customer service.

WordPress.org

WordPress.**org** is a content management system. It's the most commonly used platform for blogs and other websites. You do not need to know HTML coding to use it.

WordPress is a very flexible platform that you can customize in almost infinite ways. Many different plugins can also be added to a WordPress website. Plugins are pieces of software code that you install on your website to add new features and functions—a shopping cart, social media sharing buttons, a comment box, etc.

Step-by-step procedure

For web hosting, I personally use HostGator.com. They offer a live chat support system and a 24/7 phone line. You can get help from the technical support team at any time.

They also provide video tutorials to guide you on their YouTube channel. I mention HostGator because I have always received great service from their team, but I am *not* an affiliate. This is simply the company that I use and know best.

If you decide to choose HostGator, I have written the procedure to follow, step-by-step, from registering a domain to getting a web hosting plan and connecting it to WordPress.org. You will find the detailed procedure in the bonus material. However, if you choose BlueHost.com, which is another good option, the process should be very similar. Feel free to contact them if you need guidance in the process.

Inside WordPress.org

Once your WordPress account is created, I recommend watching the free tutorial videos from WpBeginner.com, which explain the different functions inside WordPress. Simply go to the video section of their website and register for access to the WordPress 101 series. You can also find many other free tutorials on YouTube.

You'll need to start by choosing a theme. A theme is a basic design template for your website that you'll be able to customize. Some themes are free, while others are premium and paid. I personally like the templates from ElegantThemes.com, DiyThemes.com, and ThemeForest.net, but there are many other great options. If you are looking for an easy-to-use and beautifully designed theme, I can recommend *Divi* from ElegantThemes.com.

After you have chosen and installed a theme, you'll be able to create web pages and build your entire site.

Installing plugins

To customize your website and add features, you can install numerous pieces of unique software code, called plugins. On the left sidebar of your WordPress dashboard, click on "Plugins" and "Add New." You can use the search box to find different plugins by name. There is a list of useful plugins in your bonus material.

Don't get stuck – get help!

If you still don't feel comfortable registering your domain, getting a self-hosting plan, and setting up WordPress, don't get discouraged and don't spend *hours* trying to figure everything out—just go get help!

You *do not* have to do everything yourself. You can easily find someone you know or hire a specialist to do it for you. You could also take a course to learn more about WordPress. Udemy.com, Lynda.com, and SkillShare.com offer several paid online courses on the topic. You can also find an expert in your city if you prefer to meet in person—look on Craigslist or search on Google.

It is also possible to outsource the entire process, or part of it, to a specialist for a fairly low cost. You can hire a freelancer on Fiverr.com, Freelancer.com or Upwork.com.

Just remember, don't get overwhelmed with the technical aspects of your online business. Everyone has started somewhere. You only have to be willing to learn. Furthermore, once you understand the technicalities, it isn't all that complicated!

What to Remember About the Technical Aspects

1) For an online business, a self-hosted website is recommended.

2) You'll need:
- To choose and register a domain name—your website address
- To choose a hosting plan—BlueHost, HostGator or other
- To connect the above and set up WordPress.org

3) You don't need to do everything yourself—get help. Find a course, hire someone, or ask an experienced friend to help you. Be willing to learn, but don't waste too much time on those aspects. You can also outsource part or all of the process to a freelancer.

Take Action

(Suggested time to allow for the exercise: 4 hours)

1) Think of a domain name

It can be your business name or words closely related to your topic.

- o Make sure you don't use another company's name—check if there is a trademark registered.
- o Check the availability—directly on the hosting provider (recommended) or on any other platform where you can buy and register a domain, like OnlyDomains.com or GoDaddy.com.
- o Make sure it's easy to remember, spell, and type.

2) Choose a web hosting service and select a plan

I recommend HostGator.com or BlueHost.com. Also, register your domain at the same time as purchasing a plan to avoid unnecessary confusion.

3) Create a WordPress.org account

Follow the steps mentioned in the chapter, and in the document in the bonus material.

If you have trouble doing this, get help from the support team of your hosting service, ask someone you know, or hire someone to do it for you.

CHAPTER 7

BUILDING YOUR EMAIL LIST

Why Do You Need an Email List?

Building your email list must be your number one priority, especially when you are just starting your online business.

Think of the 80/20 principle—20 percent of your effort brings 80 percent of the benefits. Building your email list is *the* action that can lead to that 80 percent.

All entrepreneurs make mistakes, but they usually don't have many regrets, because mistakes are part of the learning process. There is, however, one thing that many entrepreneurs *do* say they would have done differently if they could go back in time: start building their email list sooner.

You should start collecting emails as soon as your website has been created by offering a form where visitors can sign up.

Your Business's Number One Asset

An organization's email list is its number one asset—or, more specifically, the *relationship* that a business has with its subscribers is its number one asset.

If the 20,000 people subscribed to your list don't care about you or your product, then your list might not be worth a penny. Worse, it may be costing you money, since you pay a monthly fee to your email marketing service provider based on the number of subscribers you have. The real assets are your *engaged* email subscribers – the ones interested in buying the product or service you offer.

Remember Kevin Kelly's article, *1000 True Fans*,[3] about the importance of building a list of *quality* subscribers—people interested in buying everything you have to offer—rather than purely focusing on quantity.

In the same school of thought, email marketing guru Andre Chaperon (*AutoResponder Madness.com*) is known to have generated hundreds of thousands of dollars selling products via email with lists of fewer than 1,000 subscribers. He's a good example that what matters is the *relationship* you maintain with the people on your list.

Some marketers would argue that you are better off with a big list, and I don't disagree with them. However, what I am saying is that you're better off with a smaller list of high-quality subscribers than a huge list of people uninterested in your offer. Of course, a bigger list of quality subscribers is even better!

Here are several reasons why your email list is so important to your business:

1. You own your list.

You can have many Twitter or Pinterest followers, thousands of Facebook fans, and hundreds of subscribers to your YouTube channel, but since you don't own any of these platforms, you're not

---

[3] Article *1000 True Fans*, by Kevin Kelly

in control of your business's main asset. If Facebook or Twitter decided to shut your account down, you could lose all means of connecting and keeping in touch with your audience.

Your website, however, is yours, and so is your email list. It is, however, recommended to make regular backups of your list. Save your contacts file in an Excel document using a cloud storage service, like Dropbox, and even keep a physical copy of it. They may just be email addresses, but they're worth more than you can possibly imagine.

2. This is the most effective way to communicate with your audience.

Direct email is a personal way to communicate with your audience members, to build rapport, and to maintain your relationship with them.

Also, the most effective way to get accurate information about your audience—their needs, pains, and desires—is by surveying them, which can easily be done through email. Questioning your subscribers is a great way to find out which product or service to eventually offer.

By contacting your email subscribers regularly, you also remind them of your existence. You can send them a notification when you publish a new article and encourage them to visit your blog. You can let them know about your new product, and send them promotions.

3. Email marketing has the highest sales conversion rate.

As Derek Halpern, online marketer, says:

"Email marketing is the most cost effective and profitable way to deliver true value to an audience that wants it."

Emails are a free promotional channel through which you can reach the most targeted potential customers you could want: people who have already demonstrated an interest in your business. Not only is it a free means of advertising your product, but email marketing also has the highest sales conversion rate of any other promotional channel.

The bottom line is that building an email list of engaged subscribers will help you sell more of your product and build a stronger, more profitable business.

4. It helps to create partnerships.

Having an email list can open many doors and help you connect with other influencers in your industry. It will be easier to create partnerships because you'll have something to offer—exposure to your audience.

If you can help other businesses gain visibility within an interesting market (to them), you'll be well appreciated in your industry.

How to Build Your Email List

The process of collecting email addresses is quite simple. You need to have an opt-in form on your website for visitors to enter their information and an email marketing service to collect, store, and organize those email addresses.

Since people are reluctant to give away their personal information, you must provide them with a good reason to do so. In exchange for an email, you should offer a free gift, which we call a *lead magnet*. Let's explore these elements in more detail.

Email Marketing Service Provider

You first need to choose a system to collect the emails. An email marketing service will provide a complete system to collect email addresses and organize them, to create and automate the messages, and to split test and track your campaigns.

Most services charge a monthly fee, which usually depends on the number of subscribers you have—the cost will increase as your list grows. There are a few elements to consider when choosing an email management provider.

- **Automation:** Make sure you can automate your messages by setting a pre-determined day and time when your emails are sent to your subscribers.

- **Segmentation:** It's much better to segment people in your list according to their preferences and interests to increase the efficiency of your email campaigns. For example, you could separate people who have subscribed (and received a free eBook on exercising for weight loss) from the people who have signed up for a free Skype consultation for nutrition coaching. You can then create different email campaigns for each segment and send them offers that better correspond to their specific needs and interests.

- **A/B testing:** As we'll see in Chapter 12, testing to improve your marketing tactics is a key determinant of your business's success. A/B testing means that you send one email version (A) to half of your subscribers, and a different version (B) to the other half, and observe which version converts best. By converting, we mean the percentage of your email subscribers who opened the email or clicked a link in the email, for example. The difference between version A and B can be in the subject line, the email text, the product you're promoting, etc. Testing is how you optimize your email campaign and increase its results.

There are many email marketing service providers of varying complexity and price. Here are three that I recommend when you are just starting out:

AWeber.com

Many marketers and business owners use AWeber, since it's an affordable—yet rather complete—email management system. Its features include email automation, email marketing tracking, and subscriber segmentation. Their system is simple to use and they provide customer support seven days a week. There are also video tutorials on their website that explain the different features available.

You have access to all features, regardless of which plan you choose. The cost is only determined by the size of your list. For up to 500 subscribers, the monthly fee is $19 (at the time this book is being written), and it will increase as your list grows.

MailChimp.com

MailChimp is another popular and easy-to-use email marketing service.

Their free plan for up to 2,000 subscribers is interesting for entrepreneurs who are just starting out. While the free plan only includes some basic features, if your budget is limited, you could consider beginning with this option and then upgrading later. At least you'll be able to install a sign-up form on your website and start collecting email addresses.

To automate your emails, do A/B testing, and access the detailed data about your campaigns—all of which are determinants of your email marketing success—you'll have to upgrade to a paid plan.

MailChimp provides video tutorials explaining how to use its different features. You also have access to live customer support with the paid – but not with the free – plan.

GetResponse.com

Even with the basic plan—which starts at $15 per month—GetResponse gives you access to all the features you need when you're starting your business. Their interface is very easy to navigate, and their video tutorials are simple to understand.

They offer a 24/7 customer support live chat, as well as assistance over the phone or by email.

I personally use GetResponse because of the many features they offer and because of their appealing sign-up forms and landing pages. You can pay an extra $15/month (an add-on to the basic plan) and get access to unlimited landing pages (we'll explain what they are in a minute), which is a bargain, in my opinion.

However, all of the email marketing systems mentioned above, and many others available on the market, can be good options. You can even try them all using their free trials and then decide which one you prefer.

Your Lead Magnet

Now, let's talk about the "freebie" you'll give to your subscribers in exchange for their email address.

You've certainly seen opt-in forms that say "Subscribe to our newsletter" on many websites.

Unless the site provides incredible information that you don't want to miss out on, would you really subscribe to such a newsletter? Probably not. However, if you were offered a highly valuable free gift, such as a short video course or a practical guide, you would be much more willing to give away your email address.

For a freebie to be perceived as highly valuable, it must be something your audience really wants—or even better, needs. If you have done the research on your ideal customer's avatar in Chapter 4, then you already know what your audience's pain and desires are. Your freebie should be something that provides a solution to those issues in the same way that your paid product would.

A high-value offer doesn't mean that it has to be costly and time-consuming to produce. It simply has to solve a problem.

For example, let's say you're a fitness trainer and sell online training programs for men wishing to increase their muscle mass. Your freebie could be a cheat sheet of the five most effective exercises to build upper body muscles. Would that be useful enough information to land an email address? Of course!

To increase its perceived value, the cheat sheet could be presented in a well-designed PDF, with images to demonstrate the exercises.

A lead magnet can therefore take many forms:

- An eBook
- An audio track
- A video
- A short course
- A checklist or cheat sheet
- A free Skype consultation

The freebie could be delivered all at once, or in an email series. A series could be, for example, a short video course in three parts.

What's interesting with the series approach is that you instantly build a connection with your subscribers. They will anticipate the next email in the series and will get used to seeing your messages in their inbox.

An important element to consider when deciding on a freebie is that *it has to be relevant to your paid product.* Remember, your email subscribers are only valuable to you if they are potential customers or brand advocates.

In our previous example with the fitness trainer, the exercise cheat sheet was highly relevant to the paid product—the online fitness training programs. However, let's say the trainer thought of offering a video game as an opt-in incentive. That's not at all relevant. There is no reason to believe that the person opting-in for the video game would be interested in later purchasing fitness training. The two products aren't related.

Opt-in Form

The opt-in form is the actual form through which visitors sign up by entering their information (usually their name and email). Opt-in forms can be placed in several strategic locations on your web page to optimize the number of visitors who sign up.

Your email marketing service should provide several form templates you can easily edit and customize. It's important to choose a form that matches your brand's design and looks clean and professional.

The Text in the Form

The headline in the form should state the solution you offer and mention the freebie. Tell the visitors what they'll get after they sign up. Just under the headline, include some details about the freebie. It's a good idea to use bullet points.

For example, a headline could be "5 quick exercises to build your upper body muscles." Then, give some details about the benefits, but keep it short—the message should be easily understandable at a glance. Use large fonts and colors that match your brand, but which also stand out on the web page.

The Call-to-Action Button

The call-to-action button of the opt-in form also plays a role in the conversion. It is there to tell visitors what to do next. It's better to avoid using the boring and suspicion-inducing "Subscribe," and opt for a more benefit-oriented action verb, such as "Download Now" or "Get Instant Access." You'll also get better results by making the button stand out. Choose a contrasting color that attracts attention.

Where Do You Put the Forms on Your Website?

Little details, such as where you place the sign-up form on your web page, can lead to a huge difference in conversion in online marketing,

Since building your email list is your number one priority, your website must be designed to achieve this specific goal. There are strategic places where you should place the forms on your website to increase your chances of converting visitors into subscribers.

1. Above the fold

"Above the fold" means the portion of the webpage that the visitors see when they arrive on your site, without having to scroll down.

Using a feature box type of form—one that occupies the whole screen above the fold—works very well. This in itself should help convert many visitors into subscribers, as long as the freebie is interesting enough.

2. In the upper-right sidebar

This is probably the most common place to insert an opt-in form—at the top of your right sidebar.

3. Above the top menu

There is a free plugin you can install within WordPress called *Hello Bar* that provides a thin, horizontal form just above your website's top navigation menu.

4. After each blog post

This one is very important. A person who has read one of your articles to the bottom has demonstrated a high interest in your content. That's the type of person you want to join your email list, and you should make it easy for him/her to do so by placing an opt-in form right after the post.

You will get even better results if you offer a freebie that is relevant to the post topic. It could simply be a complement to the article, like an action plan, a checklist, or a cheat sheet.

For example, let's say that you wrote a post about content marketing. A freebie could be a list of ten compelling headline templates. If your website includes a blog, it would be a good idea to create a simple but relevant opt-in giveaway that complements your most popular articles and offers the opt-in freebie at the end of the post.

5. At the beginning of each post
A tactic that also converts well, especially if you write long blog articles, is to give readers the possibility of downloading the PDF version of the article, which they can print or save to read later. The readers simply have to enter their email addresses to download the PDF.

6. Pop-up forms
The (sometimes annoying) pop-up sign-up forms actually convert better than almost anything else. By using pop-up forms, many marketers have noticed an increase of between 30% to over 1000% in the number of daily email subscribers, in comparison to using a simple sidebar form. *WPBeginner.com* tested it on their website and found a 600% increase in their number of email subscribers.[4]

To make these pop-ups less annoying, there are a few things you can do. First, set the pop-ups to appear between ten and sixty seconds after the visitor has landed on the webpage (you can test what converts best). This way, it's less intrusive, since the visitor

---

[4] Pop-up Optimization Guide, by AWeber, http://docs.aweber-static.com/pdfs/Pop-Up-Optimization-Guide.pdf

was trying to get the information s/he was looking for, and didn't necessarily wish to be interrupted by a pop-up box right away. Another aspect that can be programmed with some pop-up software is visitor recognition. With this approach, the pop-up only appears the first time someone comes to the site, so it doesn't annoy visitors by popping up every single time. Finally, you could use an exit-intent pop-up that only appears when the visitor is about to leave the page—namely when the cursor approaches the exit tab.

Don't use pop-ups on every page of your website, because you'll quickly annoy your visitors. Simply choose to use them on a few pages that get most of your traffic.

There are several types of pop-up form software available, and three good ones are *PopUpDomination.com*, *ThriveThemes.com/leads* and *OptinMonster.com*.

Squeeze Pages

A squeeze page—also called a landing page or sales page—is a distraction-free web page to which you send traffic for a specific purpose. A specific goal, for example, could be to sell a product or collect email addresses.

We say "distraction-free" because there is no link to click, no navigation menu, and no sidebar or anything else that could take the visitor's attention away from the action you want him/her to take. There is only a call-to-action button—like "download," "sign up," or "get access"—along with a sales pitch to persuade the visitor to take action.

You can use a squeeze page as the destination page where you send people you've reached on social media or elsewhere to increase your chances of converting them into email subscribers. You can send them to the landing page, instead of your homepage, or any other page of your website.

You can create a squeeze page directly in your WordPress dashboard using a free WordPress landing page plugin. There are also more premium squeeze page builders that include more features—especially for testing and collecting data—and offer templates that are proven to convert well. A personal favorite is definitely *LeadPages.com*, but it's quite pricey. *OptimizePress.com* and *InstaPage.com* are also good options, among others.

Some email marketing management companies, like GetResponse, include squeeze pages.

Email Marketing

You've now chosen an email marketing service, created the freebie you'll offer to your site's visitors, and inserted the sign-up forms in different places on your website. Is that everything?

Well, not quite. That was Part One of your email marketing strategy—collecting those emails. Part Two is about building a relationship with your subscribers. Remember, your business's number one asset is the *relationship* you maintain with your list of subscribers.

In Part Two of your strategy you'll create a series of emails, starting with the welcome message, in which you'll give away the freebie, and continuing with other messages that will provide great value to your audience.

The goal is to make them want to open and read your emails, because if they don't, your list isn't really an asset. If no one opens your email when you're promoting a paid product, you won't make any sales!

According to research conducted by MailChimp,[5] the average email open rate is about 22%—with the best email open rate being between 60%-87%, and the worst being 1%-14%. Several factors can affect this conversion, especially:

- o The sender
  If your subscribers expect valuable information from you, they'll be more inclined to open them. Your name should be associated with "high value."

---

[5] MailChimp data: http://mailchimp.com/resources/research/

- If the message goes to the recipient's inbox or junk mail
  If a subscriber sent your message to his junk mail once, that's where your later emails will directly go as well. That's why it's important to always provide value – to avoid being sent to the junk folder. There is also a chance that even your first email will go straight to the junk mail folder. To avoid this, you should ask your subscribers to whitelist you as soon as they subscribe to your list.

- The subject line
  The subject line is meant to announce what your message is all about, and will determine if a subscriber is interested in opening the mail or not. A basic goal is to trigger interest and curiosity. To optimize the open rate, you should test different subject lines and continue using variations of what converts best. We'll explain this aspect in more detail in Chapter 12.

You can create and automate these messages in your account with an email marketing service. If you're not sure how to do it, don't worry; they all provide video tutorials that guide you through the process.

Double Opt-in Versus Single Opt-in

First of all, you must understand that you can't force or trick a person to join your list. There is legislation that protects consumers, stating that you can't add them to your list without their consent, and that you must facilitate the opt-out process for those who wish to unsubscribe.

A single opt-in means that visitors enter their email in the sign-up form and are subscribed to your list as soon as they hit the "sign-up" button. No other action is required of them; they are automatically added to your list.

A double opt-in means having to confirm your subscription. You have probably gone through the process yourself when signing up for someone's newsletter—you enter your email and are then asked to go to your inbox and confirm your subscription by clicking the link the company has sent you in the message. That's a *double opt-in* process.

It's a little longer and requires more effort from the subscriber, so you might lose some of them along the way. Not everyone will confirm their email.

Why would you choose a double opt-in process versus a single one if it means potentially losing a few subscribers?

When subscribers confirm their subscription, you lower the chances that your future messages will get sent to their spam folder. In this first message, you should even ask them to whitelist you. A double opt-in also ensures that they *do* want to join your list. You want to gain engaged subscribers, not ones that will never open your emails. Thus, this step naturally screens out potentially less engaged visitors. Finally, it is safer for you as well, since it will protect *you* against spammers.

I, and most marketers, recommend using a double opt-in process. You can increase the chance that visitors will confirm by making sure your freebie has a high perceived value.

Autoresponder Sequence

The autoresponder sequence is a series of emails you should set up to be sent to your subscribers at a pre-determined date and time. For example, you can decide that all subscribers will receive a welcome message right after they have signed up—in which they'll get the freebie—and then another message two days later, offering more useful information. Then, they could receive five other similar messages, sent every three days, for a total of seven messages. All subscribers to your list will receive the same message series at the same intervals, no matter when they sign up.

You may be wondering how many messages you should send, and how often to send them.

Unfortunately, there's no perfect answer to this, since the situation is different for each business. You'll know what works best for you over time by observing and testing. Some marketers send daily emails to their list; others send emails once a week. To help define your email sequence, ask yourself this: What is the optimal frequency that would keep the subscribers engaged and ensure they don't forget about you, without annoying them with too many messages?

Personally, I like to send the first five emails at an interval of a couple days and then once a week after that for further communication.

Sending the first few messages at a closer interval will get your subscribers accustomed to seeing you appear in their inbox. Also, sending less than one message per week for further communication would most likely weaken the relationship with your list. You want to keep your subscribers engaged and interested in your offer.

Email Content

What will you say to your subscribers?

The content of your emails must be valuable enough to make your subscribers want to open and read them. Thus, you must always provide useful information, and should vary the content of your messages to keep them interesting. Here are some examples of what you could send to your list:

- Mention a useful resource or tool
  It could be a WordPress plugin, software, a blog article, a book that you've read, or anything that you believe could help your audience achieve their goals.

- Tell a success story from a member of your audience
  This is a powerful way to prove the benefits of your product. It's also encouraging for your audience to see that others have achieved something they might be aiming for as well.

- Share a lesson you've learned to help your audience avoid making the same mistake
  This shows that you're not perfect and that it's normal to make mistakes. It also demonstrates to your audience that you care about them.

- Tell a fun fact or story
  To entertain your audience, you can also share fun facts or stories—your own or others'. This will humanize the communication and deepen the relationship with your subscribers.

- Ask them a question
    This is a great way to get information about your audience and encourage them to participate in the conversation. You can ask about their main problems or desires, ask them to share their opinions, etc.

- Announce a promotion
    Your email subscribers should always get the best deals on your products or services. If you are discounting one of your products, make sure they know about the deal before anyone else.

- Sell a product (your own or an affiliate's)
    You should also be selling something in your emails. This could be the main purpose of a message or be subtly announced within the email.

    Many marketers softly promote their paid products at the end of their message, saying something like, "P.S. By the way, if you're interested in learning X, I've got a product Y that you may find interesting…" and then link to the product sales page—a squeeze page with the sole objective of generating sales.

    You don't have to sell something in every email, but you should do it often enough that your subscribers become accustomed to it. You should feel comfortable doing this, so don't wait too long before offering a paid product!

    If you don't have a product of your own yet, you can promote someone else's. It can be as simple as a book that you recommend, for which you'll get a commission for every sale.

For books, this can be very easily done through the Amazon affiliate program. Even if you won't make considerable income from this, the real goal is to get your subscribers used to seeing paid products being announced.

Note: You legally have to tell people about an affiliate product that you promote by mentioning that you get a sales commission—but at no extra cost to them.

Treat Your Subscribers Like Friends

Never forget what your email subscribers are—real people. Craft your messages as if you were sending them to your friends. Use a conversational tone, and demonstrate a genuine desire to help.

Most email marketing services will allow you to personalize your messages by automatically adding the real name of every subscriber. This is why you're often asked to enter your name along with your email address when filling in a sign-up form. Simple details like this will make your communication more personal.

You can tell your subscribers not to hesitate to reply to your messages and to contact you if they have any questions. If you offer this, try to reply to every message. This will be easier to do while your list is small, obviously.

Of course, it will all have to be done genuinely!

What's Next?

Now that you have a whole system in place to build, nurture, and grow your business's main asset—your email list—there is only one thing that you're missing: traffic to your website.

To gain subscribers, you must first have visitors. In the next chapter, we'll talk about ways to drive traffic to your site.

What to Remember About Building an Email List

1) The relationship you maintain with your email subscribers is your business's number one asset. Building your list should be your priority.

2) You'll need to sign up with an email marketing service, which will allow you:
- o   To create sign-up forms and collect email addresses
- o   To segment your list
- o   To create and automate messages
- o   To split test and collect data for optimizing your email campaigns.

3) You can place the forms in different locations on your web page to maximize the conversion of visitors into subscribers.

4) You'll have to create a freebie as an incentive for visitors to subscribe to your list. This free gift must:
- o   Have a high perceived value to your audience, and preferably solve a problem they have.
- o   Be related to your paid product or service.

5) You must maintain the relationship with your subscribers by continually sending them messages that provide useful information. You can automate these messages, or send them punctually.

Take Action

(Suggested time to allow for the exercise: 5 hours)

1) Choose an email marketing service.

Subscribe to a few services' free trials, and select the one you prefer.

2) Create a freebie to offer to your subscriber.

- Think of something useful and of high value that can solve a problem related to your audience's pain or desire.
- Decide on how you'll package your freebie: audio, PDF, video or other. Will it be a one-time download or will it be sent in a series?
- If you have a blog, try to create a simple freebie relevant to each of your best—and most popular—pieces of content.

3) Create a sign-up form.

- Choose a form design that matches your brand
- Clearly mention the freebie and the associated benefits
- Place it in several locations on your webpages

4) Craft the first few messages of your email series.

- Start with the welcome message, in which you also give subscribers the free gift
- Write another five to ten messages to be sent in the following days and weeks. Always provide value and be useful.

CHAPTER 8

GETTING TRAFFIC TO YOUR WEBSITE

A common analogy in online business is that, without traffic (visitors coming to your site), your website is like a billboard in the middle of the desert. Even if you write the most interesting posts, create the best products, or offer an outstanding service, if no one knows about it, your business won't get very far.

Driving traffic to your new business website can often seem like the biggest roadblock of your online business journey. However, once you have managed to get through this stage, everything will be easier.

Today, with millions of websites online, it has become increasingly difficult for new businesses to appear on the first page of search engine results. You can't rely solely on search engine traffic when you're just starting out. You have to find other ways to drive potential customers to your website.

Just to clarify, when we say "driving traffic to your *website*," note that this could be to *any* destination you wish to send people to.

I highly recommend that you create your *own* website, as it will be yours and you'll be in control of what happens there. Your website is like your home. However, instead of "website" we could also use the term "platform," as it could be a podcast that you host, a

YouTube channel, an Etsy store where you sell products, or anywhere else you wish to drive traffic.

Now, let's see what can be done to attract some eyeballs to your website—or wherever you wish to send visitors to engage with your offer.

First of All, Where Is Your Target Audience Hanging Out?

Think back to your ideal customer's avatar.

If you haven't done the earlier exercise about defining your niche and understanding your audience (Chapters 3 and 4), you'll have to go back before moving forward.

Why? Because when you're just starting—and thus, don't have an existing audience—the best way to build one is by showing up in places where they already hang out. In order to know where to find them, you have to know who they are. Think about it: a 65-year-old ex-military grandfather doesn't visit the same websites and read the same blogs as a 22-year-old Fine Arts college student. It's that simple.

You have to go back to your ideal customers' profiles. Who are they? What are they interested in? What websites and blogs do they visit and read? What social media platforms do they use?

Aim for "Quality" Traffic

It's important to know who your ideal customer is because you want to drive quality traffic to your website, namely, potential buyers of your product or service.

A bigger site with more traffic doesn't necessarily generate more sales than a smaller site with less traffic. It all depends on the *quality* of the traffic, which is measured by:

- **Engagement:** visitors commenting on and sharing your blog posts, for example
- **Conversion:** visitors subscribing to your email list, or ending up, at some point, buying your product or service
- **Brand advocates:** visitors talking about you to their friends and acquaintances

Basically, do your visitors contribute to your business growth?

Of course, as we've said before, it's even better if you can get a good quantity of quality traffic. So, how do you get high-quality traffic?

It's quite simple. You have to reach the people who are most likely to be interested in your content—posts, videos, audio—and in buying your product or service. These people are your target audience.

Is Your Website Ready to Welcome Visitors?

The main sections of your website

Before you even try to get visitors to your website, you must be ready to welcome them with the information they're seeking.

Your website should contain at least three sections—four if you have a blog, and five if you also have a product to sell.

1) A Homepage
   At a glance, your homepage should clearly state what you're offering—information on your product or service—and whom the offer is for.

2) An "About" page
   This section contains information on you and your business, but more specifically about "what's in it for *them*." We'll explain the *purpose* of the "About page" in more detail in Chapter 11.

3) A "Contact" page
   Give visitors a way to contact you to get more information.

4) A blog section
   Your website might be a blog or contain a blog section, where you'll publish articles, videos, or content in other formats. In that case, it should contain at least a few articles.

5) A sales page
   If you already have a product or service to sell, you should also have a sales page in place.

Be Useful

Especially if your website is a blog—or contains a blog—before you drive traffic to it, you should have at least two or three *great* pieces of published content that are closely related to the product or service you are selling—or planning to offer in the future. It could be a written article, a video, or a "how to" guide, as long as it provides useful information that (ideally) solves a problem.

Even if you are not planning on writing a blog, it would still be wise to produce these two or three pieces of content, as they will demonstrate your expertise and desire to help. For example, a nutrition coach offering online consultation could write two or three articles about specific healthy habits. Simply think of something useful to share with your target market that is relevant to your main offer.

A Blog Section

If your website is a blog, driving traffic is not your only concern—you'll also want the visitors to be engaged and to come back. To do this, you'll have to provide original and high-quality content.

What is good content?

According to an analysis by *Buzzsumo.com*, longer content (2000+ words) gets better ranking in the search engines, as well as more engagement. However, some prominent bloggers recommend shorter articles, averaging no more than 500 words. Michael Hyatt, author of the book *Platform: Get Noticed In A Noisy World*, states that shorter posts tend to get more comments and shares.

You could experiment with both approaches, for example, by writing one shorter post per week, and one longer and more in-depth article every month. Whichever approach you choose, create content that offers a solution to one specific problem.

The design of your content also plays a huge role—consistent fonts, along with appealing images, will increase the perceived quality of the article.

At that point, you'll also have to promote your content. You can't expect potential readers to just accidentally find your articles. Derek Halpern, founder of *SocialTriggers.com*, used this formula (with great results) during the first months of launching his website: *"Spend 20% of your time creating content and 80% promoting it."*

The bottom line is, you don't have to be writing a new blog post every day. It will be more effective to write fewer, but very interesting and valuable, pieces of content, and then put more effort into promoting them.

Traffic Sources

When you're just starting out, trying to be everywhere is overwhelming—and unnecessary. After going through the list below, choose a few traffic-generation methods—maybe two or three—that could attract the highest number of quality visitors to your site.

Make sure to use the 80/20 rule. What are the 20% of all traffic sources that will potentially bring you the 80% of your highly targeted visitors? You can always expand your efforts later. Initially, it's better to promote well through a few channels, rather than make an average effort in many channels. Choose the best traffic sources, according to your topic, your niche, and the nature of your product or service.

Here's an example that illustrates this idea:

A friend of mine recently started creating jewelry and selling it on the Internet through a store on *Etsy.com*. Her jewelry is delicate, made of gold and silver, and is sold for between $15 and $50 per piece. Her target audience is middle-class women between the ages of 25 and 40 who like low-cost accessories. Where should she primarily promote her product?

Probably on Facebook, Pinterest and fashion blogs. She should create a Facebook page because it's the social media platform with the most users, and should rarely be ignored. There's also an Etsy app that she could add to her Facebook page to send visitors directly to her Etsy store. Facebook also allows posts with large images, which is good for a product that's easily communicated visually.

Secondly, it would be almost impossible to ignore Pinterest. Pinterest's audience is made up of roughly 70% women, it's a visual medium, and it has a high sales conversion rate (the percentage of people who buy a product after visiting the platform). The pinned images are clickable, which makes it possible to send traffic directly to her website or to *Etsy.com*.

Finally, she should consider approaching fashion bloggers. Since jewelry is an accessory that complements clothing well, she could propose a partnership and be featured on a fashion blog. This would be very targeted, as there is a good chance that people who visit fashion blogs are interested in jewelry, as well. It would also be less expensive to create these partnerships with other bloggers in her industry than to advertise on high-traffic websites.

With just these three traffic sources, she could probably reach a good number of potential buyers.

Now, we'll explore several strategies to drive traffic to your website and promote your offer. As always, choose the best options for *your* business.

1. Guest post on other blogs.

"Guest posting" means writing and publishing an article on someone else's blog or website. Both the writer and the publisher can benefit from this practice.

As the author of the article, you'll get a link back to your website—usually in the author bio box at the end of the article—which can drive traffic to your site.

The goal is to write for a blog that has a medium-to-large audience that corresponds with your target customers. You get exposure in front of a new audience with the aim of growing your business.

As for the publishing site, it gets a piece of good-quality content that is useful for its audience for free. Many bloggers will accept contributors to their site since it diminishes the workload of constantly creating new and fresh content.

The main difficulty with this method is that popular blogs receive tons of requests from aspiring guest writers. Everyone wants to get more exposure by being featured on high-traffic blogs. You'll have to convince the blog owners to choose *you* over others.

However, since guest posting is one of the most effective ways to drive highly targeted traffic to your website, the hustle is really worth it. Here are some steps you might want to follow:

1) Identify blogs related to your topic that also share the same audience (niche market) as yours.

Make two lists—one with sites that have a medium-sized audience, and one with sites that have a very large audience, such as the *Huffington Post*. Make sure they accept contributors and that not just the blog owners themselves write all of the articles.

2) Find out which specific topics are the most popular within the audience of the site you wish to write for.

The article you write for the host site must be very interesting and useful to the site's audience. To identify which topics are popular among the audience, look for those that got the most shares, likes and comments.

Some blogs also have a list of their most popular posts displayed on the right sidebar. Using this information to guide your submission will increase your chances of being selected by the blog owner and driving traffic back to your website.

Remember, you should also write about topics relevant to *your* business, and even to the product or service that you sell.

Don't get me wrong, you wouldn't insert a sales pitch or any other promotional messages into your article. Simply keep in mind that, at the end of the day, what you want is to drive traffic to your site to gain email subscribers and potential customers. The best article will be one that satisfies the other site's audience *and* your objectives.

3) Observe the blogger's style.

Not only should you choose a topic that has the best chances of interesting the blogger's audience, but you should also try to write an article in the same format as what's already been published and attracted the most interest.

Are the posts mainly written in a list or a bullet-point format? Do they tell stories? Is the tone humorous or serious? Are they more in the "how to" format?

4) Build rapport with the medium-sized blog owners on the list you made.

It is important to make these connections before requesting to be featured. It can take some time to build rapport, but here are some effective ways to do it:

- o Comment on their blog posts
- o Share their articles with your social media followers

- Follow and even mention or re-tweet the blogger, when appropriate, on Twitter (using @TheirUserName)
- Comment on their Facebook page
- Subscribe to their email list and reply to an email they have sent that you've found particularly useful to thank them (don't overdo it)

But be genuine, not spammy! Only comment when you really have something to add to the conversation, and share content when it triggered something strong enough within you to do so.

5) Request to publish an article on those medium-audience blogs.

If you're subscribed to their lists, reply to a message they've sent to communicate with them instead of sending a new message—it is more likely to get their attention.

Explain the information you think their audience could benefit from that you would like to share in an article. Also, provide them with the link to your website so they know who you are and can see samples of your writing.

Reassure them by mentioning that you'll have the article proofread and will send it in a ready-to-publish format. You should also mention the number of words your article will contain and ensure that it follows the usual blog format.

6) Use your publishing experiences on smaller sites to approach blogs with a larger audience.

The blogs with a very large audience and high traffic, such as the *Huffington Post*, have a team of editors who receive thousands of requests from writers to be published. By simply submitting your article the regular way, it will probably end up going unnoticed. A better way is to directly contact the editors in charge of the section related to your topic. It helps if you've previously built a rapport with them, and Twitter is probably the most appropriate channel for this—start by following the editors and retweeting some of their content.

2. Accept guest writers on your blog.

Another way to increase your exposure and gain traffic is by allowing another person to write an article on *your* website. This time, the topic of the article must be interesting to *your* audience.

You then get exposure by asking the contributor to share the link to the article in his/her network by providing it in his/her email list and on social media. This way, every time someone clicks the link to read the post, they end up on *your* website.

3. Get interviewed on podcasts.

Another excellent way to gain exposure is by getting interviewed on a podcast. The same rule applies here—the podcast audience must be similar to your target audience. You need to have some expertise, valuable experience, or information to share that will be interesting to the podcast listeners if you want to be interviewed.

The first step is to find podcasts on your topic through the iTunes store. Listen to a few of them and find the shows you believe you could bring value to by being interviewed.

Then, start connecting with the show host. Review the show, comment on the website, if there is one, and follow the host on Twitter before requesting an interview. The same is true as with guest posting—at first, you'll have a better chance of being featured on smaller shows. You'll know the importance of a podcast by the caliber of guests being interviewed. If the guests are bestselling authors or very influential people, the show must be very important.

Opt for the smaller ones to start and leverage this experience to get interviews on more important shows.

4. Interview an expert in your field.

Interviewing experts is a great strategy to generate traffic, build relationships with influencers, and gain authority in your field. You can present these interviews on your website, in a text or an audio format, or both.

Not only can it be very interesting for your audience to get the opportunity to learn from the experts, but these experts will most likely share the interview with their social media followers, which can generate more traffic to your site.

You can find experts in your field by searching for your topic on Google, LinkedIn, Twitter or other social media platforms. You can also look for university teachers or affluent people in your community.

Once you've made a good list of potential interviewees, conduct research on them. Find out about their experience, the articles they have written, and the shows on which they've appeared.

When you contact them, state the reasons why your audience could really benefit from their expertise. Also, mention what's in it for *them*, the interviewees. For example, exposure to a new audience, or the opportunity to share useful information with the community. Then, contact them through email, LinkedIn or Twitter.

5. Host webinars.

Webinars are basically seminars held online. They're like live workshops.Usually, they last around one to two hours. They can be used to promote a product, to generate sales, or to build an audience. They can be free, or imply a cost to attend.

At this stage in your business, the main objective of a webinar is to generate traffic to your website and build your email list, not to generate revenue. Therefore, it should be free to attend, and it's also better not to promote a paid product or service right away—you want to reach a new audience and build a trusting relationship with them, not make them feel like they're going to be "pitched."

The webinar host (you) will make a presentation on a specific topic. Of course, you need to have some expertise, skills, or knowledge to share that's useful to others. It's even better if the information you provide solves a problem. Your presentation can be in a video format, or can be made using PowerPoint or Keynote slides.

To host a webinar, you'll need to use a platform like *Go To Webinar, Webinar Jam* or *Webinars On Air.* You simply register, enter your information, and follow the instructions. The software will generate a link, which you'll give when promoting the webinar so that people can register and get access to it.

Make sure you understand how the system works before planning your first event. Most webinar platforms provide free tutorials explaining the process.

I know what you're wondering now—how do you get people to sign up? There are two main ways to get people to sign up for your webinar:

1. Promote it through someone else's audience.

If you have valuable information to share, it shouldn't be too hard to convince someone in your industry to promote your webinar with his/her audience. Hint: Don't pick a direct competitor, but rather someone who offers a product or service that is complementary to yours.

2. Promote with advertising and on social media.

You can promote your free webinar on social media, such as in Facebook or LinkedIn groups of which you are a member. You can also use Pinterest and Twitter, or any other social media, depending on your target audience. For Twitter, make sure to properly use hashtags with keywords related to the webinar topic to ensure that your tweet will be found.

You can also use Facebook ads to promote the webinar. With Facebook ads, you can target people who have liked the pages of companies similar to yours. This is more effective, since they are people who have already demonstrated an interest in your topic. In 2015, Facebook launched a new ad campaign feature, called *lead ads*. It makes it easier, faster and more effective to collect leads (subscribers), have them sign up to your webinar or email list, or to take any other action. Online business owners should definitely take advantage of this new, powerful feature.

You could also use search engine advertising to appear in the commercial links of Google search results (Google AdWords). The commercial links are the first few that appear at the top of the results page. This system is based on bidding— you'll compete against other companies for the keywords that will be shown to other users. If you're not careful, it can get very pricey. Before you think of using Google AdWords, make sure you fully understand how it works.

Another way to promote your webinar is through *MeetUp.com*. *MeetUp.com* is more about face-to-face meetings, but I'm a member of a few groups that have hosted live webinars as part of their event series. If you become a member of a group related to your topic, you could propose holding a free webinar to share useful information with the group.

As mentioned, you probably shouldn't sell anything during this webinar. However, you should collect email addresses from the people who signed up and mention your website—and even direct people to it for more information—during the session. That's how you'll generate traffic to your site.

6. Build a community on social media.

It's very easy to feel overwhelmed with social media, so remember—you don't have to be everywhere!

Big companies and highly prominent bloggers that are active on all social platforms usually have a virtual assistant to help them. Until you can hire an assistant, focus on a couple of platforms, learn how to use them in depth, develop an audience, and then, once you're well established, explore other platforms.

Once again, choose the media that are the most relevant to your audience, your topic, and the nature of your product or service. Generally, Facebook should be one of the platforms you choose, simply because most people use it. Facebook is a very versatile platform—you can upload videos, audio tracks, images and text—and it has many integrated functions you can use to promote your business.

To help you figure out where your target audience is, look for social media user demographic reports. *Pew Research Center* publishes such reports.

Another great tool to help you choose the right platforms is *Buzzsumo.com*. Once on the Buzzsumo website, search for keywords related to your topic. You can then see how many shares the most popular pieces of content written on the topic have had on each social medium. You'll want to use the platforms in which the content related to your topic gets shared the most.

Since every business is different, I'll only briefly present the most popular social media platforms. Once you've found the most appropriate medium for your business, learn as much about it as possible.

You can listen to tutorials on *YouTube.com*, read articles on *SocialMediaExaminer.com*, listen to the *Social Media Marketing Podcast* in the iTunes store, or take a course on *SkillShare.com* or *Udemy.com*. It's all worth it—knowing how to use social media effectively will help you get more exposure much faster.

Facebook

"With 1.49 billion users, Facebook has more monthly active users than WhatsApp (500 million), Twitter (284 million) and Instagram (200 million) — combined."[6] Perhaps you understand why Facebook cannot be ignored and should be one of your channels of choice.

As a business owner, there are several interesting aspects of Facebook that can be used to build a community, generate traffic and grow your email list. A company page is the most common way

---

[6] Source: CNBC

to connect with an audience. You can also create a Facebook group, along with a page. Note that you would still need a company page, as it'll be the only way to use advertising.

What's interesting with a group, however, is the stronger sense of community it creates. In a group, people have to request to become a member, and it's more intimate, so there is usually more engagement and participation from members. A group is also a great way to inquire about the struggles and desires of your target audience, mainly by asking them questions, and to build a stronger connection with them.

To let Facebook users know about the existence of *your* group, you can mention it in other related groups of which you are a member, and also use the advertising function through your Facebook page.

The "events" function can be used to announce webinars or other online activities to your fans and members of your group. Use the call-to-action button on your company's page (next to the "like" button) to invite people to sign up to your email list. This will redirect them to a sign-up form on your website.

There are several other apps you can add to your page, such as an Etsy tab, which sends people interested in your product directly to your Etsy store. To find an app, enter a term—for example "Etsy"—in the Facebook search box, and select "app." Then, simply install it.

Lastly, once you have created a company page, you can use Facebook advertising to reach an audience. Facebook allows businesses to create highly targeted ad campaigns. You can target:

- o The people liking your company's page (your fans)
- o An audience similar to your company's fans, crafted by Facebook's system
- o An audience sharing a particular interest, or according to their geographic location
- o The people liking your competitors' pages—there is a good chance they will be interested in your company as well

Some advanced functions also allow you to import the emails of your email list and target your ads to those people (as long as they have a Facebook account and the email is the same they used to register that account). As not everyone always opens the emails you'll send, targeting them on Facebook can ensure a wider reach for your message.

Finally, another advanced feature is retargeted ads—you can target your ads to people who have previously visited a particular page on your website. For example, if you advertise a product that you offer, you could show the ad to visitors that have viewed that product's sales page on your website, but haven't bought.

With all that said, you might wonder how much advertising can cost on Facebook. That's for you to decide. At the beginning, a good rule of thumb is to invest about five dollars per ad set, just to test and get used to the system. Once you are more comfortable in crafting your ads (choosing the right headline, image and call-to-action), you could spend about $20/day for a week or so and then measure the results to see if your strategy was worth it.

Twitter

Apart from sharing content, Twitter is also a great place to connect with influential people in your field. Even though you'll probably never get the phone numbers of big players in your industry, you can get their attention on Twitter more easily than on most other social platforms using the functions hashtag (#) and @.

When you use a hashtag in front of a term inside a tweet, your content will be shown to people who are searching for this term, even if they don't follow you. When you don't use hashtags, only your followers will see your tweets. Thus, for more exposure, always use hashtags. If you want to get someone's attention, use @ in front of the twitter username of that person. It's a bit like "poking."

Twitter can be a great place to build relationships with people in your field and to eventually get your content shared by others.

If you've written a great piece of content in which you quote someone influential, it's worth letting that person know by using the @, as there's a good chance s/he will retweet your content to his/her own followers, which will increase the exposure of your article.

Lastly, a good way to build connections on Twitter is by participating in Twitter chats. These are live chats, often compared to networking events, in the comfort of your home, using your keyboard. There are chats on many topics—you can find the schedule on sites like *ChatSalad.com*. Watch a Twitter chat tutorial on YouTube to learn how they work.

Pinterest

Many entrepreneurs have started using Pinterest to get traffic, as it can be very effective. Pinterest users are mainly women (roughly 70%), but the male segment is constantly growing in size.

This is a very easy-to-use social platform, and it doesn't require much time. You should really consider using this media if your product or service is well communicated visually—design, art, fashion, home decor, accessories, cooking, travel, etc.

One main aspect that differentiates Pinterest from Instagram is the possibility to embed a link in your images (pins) and send people directly to your website, or wherever else you want to drive traffic to.

Another interesting aspect of the platform is the possibility to become a member of a board group. Groups often have thousands of members, and by becoming a member, you largely increase the visibility of your pins (your content). You can find a list of board groups on *PinGroupie.com*.

There is also a paid promotion feature on Pinterest that makes your pins get more exposure, and help you grow your following.

Like any other social platform, Pinterest is a community. People will "repin" your content if it's worth repinning and if you've previously interacted with them by liking and sharing *their* content.

Lastly, since 90% of its users interact with the platform through the mobile app, you should create vertical images, and use large and clear fonts, to ensure that your images stand out and get noticed.

Instagram

Instagram is an online mobile app used to share photos and videos. Like Pinterest, it's a visual medium, so making your content visually appealing is the key to sparking people's interest. Content that triggers emotions tends to get higher engagement from users.

On Instagram, you first need to build your following, and then you can encourage your followers to visit your website. The way to send traffic to your website with Instagram is by adding its link in your bio section. You should include a strong call to action, such as "Get a free eBook by clicking this link," in your profile and in the description of the images or videos you share. Ideally, you should send viewers to a page on your website created to collect their email addresses—a squeeze page.

To get more followers, you'll have to share content—images and videos—regularly. Even share multiple times a day for better results.

Use hashtags in front of the keywords you would like to be found for in the *comment* section—not in the description. Using hashtags, you get the chance to be found by users that aren't your followers (yet), but who are searching for these terms in the search box.

Another way to gain more followers is by following users that may potentially be interested in your business—they might follow you back. For example, think of your competitors' followers. The users following your competitors might also like your content.

To find your competitors' followers, use the *CrowdFireApp.com* tool. Once you register, click on "Copy Followers" in the left sidebar, and enter the competitor's Instagram username. The tool will generate the list of its followers, who you can follow.

Lastly, request "shout outs" from other users with a big following (over 100,000 followers). This is a type of advertising through a free or paid agreement between two Instagram users when one mentions the other. You'll want to get "shout outs" from users who share the same target audience as yours.

Before using these tactics to gain followers, you'll need to have some content published to give a reason for people to follow you. Also, don't forget that Instagram is first and foremost a social networking channel. Interact with other brands and users by commenting on *their* content as well.

YouTube

YouTube is the second-largest search engine after Google. It has over a billion users.

The video format allows for a more intimate connection with an audience, since people can see you and hear your voice. Many entrepreneurs are intimidated by being in front of the camera, and by the technical aspects of recording and editing videos. If you feel comfortable enough to use this format, it could help you stand out from others in your field.

As for the technical aspects, they shouldn't be very difficult, nor do you need expensive equipment. You can film with your computer's webcam or with your smartphone, and then edit the video on the YouTube platform, which is quite simple to do.

The only thing you will want to spend some money on right from the beginning is a good microphone. Sound quality will affect the overall perceived quality of your videos. A couple of options, among others, are Blue Yeti and Audio-Technica Lavalier microphones. It's also best to record in a soundproof room.

For your videos to be found on YouTube, you'll have to optimize their title, tags, and description. If you integrate the proper terms (keywords) related to your video in these sections, you'll have a good chance of appearing in the search results when someone is searching for those terms.

Then, by using annotations—embedded links—in your videos, you can direct viewers to your website.

LinkedIn

Depending on your industry, LinkedIn could be a good platform to help you get traffic and subscribers.

To build relationships on LinkedIn—connections or followers—you'll first need to fill out your profile and make it stand out.

Many see LinkedIn as a place to upload their resume, but remember that it's a social media platform, and social media are used to facilitate connections with other human beings. People like to connect with people, and even more so with people they can relate to. In other words, don't be shy about showing a bit of your personality and mentioning some of your main interests.

One way to build connections and get more followers is by becoming a member of groups. You can search for groups related to your field and request to join. If you participate by commenting, asking and answering questions, and sharing useful information, you'll get noticed by other members of the group. You're allowed to post links to your blog or website, just as you would in a Facebook group. LinkedIn groups can be a great place to start building relationships with people in your field.

Another way to get noticed on LinkedIn is by commenting on articles on Pulse (LinkedIn's blog section). When commenting, add value to the conversation by sharing your opinions and knowledge, instead of just saying "Great article!" This way, you might get some people to follow you.

You could also publish your own articles on this platform to show your expertise and attract followers.

7. SlideShare Presentations

SlideShare.net is owned by LinkedIn. It's a platform where you can upload your own and view others' PowerPoint presentations—or Keynote presentations, for Mac—in a PDF format. These presentations can be viewed on *SlideShare.net*, shared on social media or embedded in a website.

SlideShare presents information in an easy-to-digest format: a small amount of text with reinforcing images. What could a presentation contain? It could be, for example, the main aspects discussed in a blog post presented in a more concise form, using bullet points. The key is to create a highly visual presentation that will attract users' attention and provide useful information. For brand awareness, consider inserting your logo in a corner of your slides.

When you upload a presentation, you have the option of entering keywords. These keywords will allow your presentation to be found on *SlideShare.net*.

You can also insert a link back to your website on the slides. That's how you'll drive traffic. For better results, the link should be inserted at the beginning, in the middle, and at the end of the presentation. You should also offer an incentive—like a free PDF document that gives more details about the topic discussed in your SlideShare presentation—to encourage viewers to click on the link.

Many business owners and bloggers have said that this platform generates more engaged traffic than other social media. For "business-to-business" companies, it can be as much as five times more important. This is quality traffic, since the presentation viewers have already demonstrated an interest in your content or offer.

8. Forums

Participating on forums related to your topic can drive highly targeted traffic, *if* the forum allows you to add a link to your website when responding to a thread. Make sure you read the forum guidelines before participating.

When you find a good forum related to your topic, fill out your profile completely. Forums are a community, which means they are based on trust and respect. For a few days, simply comment without including your link.

Then, begin responding to questions you know the answer to. In your answer, add a link to a page or a post on your website that provides useful information on the topic related to the question. Even better, you could write an article answering a question asked in a popular thread and then give the link to it. However, remember that forums aren't the place for a sales pitch—simply provide useful information.

To find a forum, you can do a Google search ("forum + your topic"), or search through the many forum directories, like *ProBoards.com*.

There are other sites very similar to forums that you could also look at, such as:

- Yahoo! Answers
- *Answers.com*
- Yahoo! Groups
- *Quora.com* (Hint: on Quora, look at the related questions on the right sidebar next to each question thread)

9. Amazon Kindle Store

By writing and self-publishing a book, you can get considerable traffic from the Amazon Kindle store. The book doesn't have to be 250 pages long—fifty or seventy pages on a specific topic is good enough, as long as it's well written and provides useful information.

Think about it—self-publishing a book is like writing a very long blog post and putting it in front of millions of potential readers! Well, maybe *millions* won't be interested in your specific topic, but your content will have much more exposure than if you simply publish it on your new website.

To ensure that your book is found by as many readers as possible, I recommend that you learn about Kindle publishing and the marketing strategies around it. You will discover a whole new world of possibilities! Not only can you drive traffic to your website and get readers to subscribe to your email list—typically by offering bonus material—but you'll also build your authority and gain credibility in your field. This is a strategy that many have already used successfully.

To learn more about Amazon self-publishing, I recommend that you begin by listening to Steve Scott's (free) podcast, *Self-Publishing Questions*, available on iTunes.

10. Social Bookmarking Sites

If you have a blog, you could submit your articles to bookmarking sites like *Delicious.com*, *Digg.com* and *StumbleUpon.com*.

First, sign up for an account, fill in your profile, and choose the categories in which you are interested. Bookmarking sites are also communities, so you'll need to share, comment, and vote on other bloggers' articles.

To publish your own posts, simply submit the article you would like to share by copying and pasting the link to it in the box provided for this purpose. The community votes on the submitted content, so if yours gets a lot of votes, you'll have a chance to appear on the front page of the platform… which will likely drive tons of traffic to your site! It really doesn't take more than a few minutes—even seconds—to submit a link to your article.

11. Search Engine Optimization (SEO)

While it's true that you can't rely solely on search engines to drive traffic to your website, especially at the beginning, that doesn't mean you shouldn't already optimize the aspects you have control over to increase your site's chances of eventually appearing in search engine results. This process is part of "search engine optimization" (SEO).

Note that we'll use Google as our consistent search engine example, since it is the engine of choice for more than 80% of all Internet users.

First, it's good to remember what Google's goal is. Like any respectable company, Google wants to serve its customers—the search engine users—well. It wants to provide the best possible results and the best answer to its users' queries.

Thus, you should only aim to rank for the right terms (keywords) that are relevant to your specific piece of content or web page.

Mainly, SEO can be divided into two categories: on-site and off-site.

The part you have the most control over is your on-site optimization. This is everything you can do to your website itself to rank better.

- **Choosing the right keywords**

    Keywords are terms that you use to describe your business and any piece of content you publish online. You need to use them properly so they can be found on the Web by people searching for those terms. Keywords tell the search engines that you might have the answer to an Internet user's query.

    With the hundreds of millions of websites online, there is fierce competition to rank in search engines. To get a chance of appearing within the first search results, you must aim for keywords with lower competition, but that still have a considerable search volume.

    To give you an example, the keyword "online business" is far too competitive for a new website to have any chance of appearing in the Google search results. Therefore, you must look for alternative keywords, especially for what we call "long tail keywords," which are keyword phrases of three or more words.

    For example, "starting an online business" or, even better, "starting an online business for beginners." These are more specific, and therefore much less competitive. Tools like

141

Soovle.com and *KeywordTool.io*, can give you an idea of keyword phrases that users look for in search engines, and help you choose some effective long tail terms.

But how do you know which keywords are good (high search volume and low competition)?

Well, to get this information, you'll need a more premium tool—a keyword analysis tool. Most of these cost money, but *SemRush.com* will give you the information on volume and competition for a *few* keywords for free. To get more results, along with access to other features, you will have to upgrade to a paid version. Another good tool that generates less competitive keyword phrases is *LongTailPro.com*.

Keyword analysis tools are pricey, but it is worth investing in one once you can afford it. It will help you generate the best terms to use in your website pages, posts, images, etc. If you can't afford a tool like this at the moment, you could hire someone on *Fiverr.com*, for five dollars, to conduct some simple keyword research.

- **Choosing a relevant domain name**

    It's a great idea to use a domain name that includes your main keywords. If you can find such a domain available, take it! If not, at least go for a simple domain name that's easy to remember, without numbers and with the least number of hyphens possible. Those domains are more SEO friendly.

- **Using the headline codes H1, H2, H3**

  H1 code is for a title (of a website page or post), H2 is for a headline, and H3 is for a sub-headline. H1 is already taken care of in WordPress (title section). What you need to make sure to use are H2 and H3. Simply highlight the text corresponding to your headlines and tag it H2 in the paragraph section of your writing editor under "paragraph" in WordPress. You can do the same for the sub-headlines, by selecting H3. Those tags make the titles and headlines more noticeable by the search engine.

- **Optimizing your page and posting titles**

  Your page and post titles should also contain your main keyword phrase, and it's more effective when those terms are the first ones in the title. For example, if using the keyword phrase "starting an online business," a page titled "Starting an Online Business for Beginners: A Complete Guide" is better than "A Complete Guide for Starting an Online Business."

- **Using your main keyword phrase at the beginning of the post**

  Your keyword phrase should be mentioned within the first one hundred words of your post or page text.

- **Verifying the keyword density of your pages and posts**

  Note that this process isn't about stuffing your text with keywords. They only serve to tell Google what your article is about. If your page or post contains your keyword too many times, Google might actually punish you—and believe me, you don't want that!

You don't want to be seen as a spammer, right? You should therefore verify your keyword density. There is a free tool, *WordCounter.net*, in which you can copy and paste your text and see how many times certain terms are mentioned. With over 3% density (3 times a term for every 100-word text), Google can penalize you. It's best to aim for a 2% keyword density.

- **Optimizing your images**

    Images can't be read by search engines, so you have to fill in their title, description, and ALT text using the same keywords once they've been uploaded into WordPress. Even the image file should be named by the keyword phrase before you upload it into WordPress.

- **Optimizing your URL permalinks**

    Just under a post or a page title in the WordPress editor, there's a permalink. You can edit the link and once again use the keywords, separated by hyphens. For example, starting-an-online-business. Note that once you have published the page or post, you must not modify the permalink again.

- **Using anchor links appropriately inside your text**

    The most important factors considered by Google to determine which sites show up in the search results are *links*. We've already talked about the domain name and the permalinks, but there are also the relevant links between different pages of your website.

    For example, imagine that you've written a post about yoga poses and another about breathing exercises, and have mentioned the importance of breathing properly in the post about yoga. You could then use a hyperlink on the phrase mentioning the importance of breathing, in the yoga poses article, to link it to the breathing exercises article. This type of link can be created directly in the WordPress editor. The key here is *relevance*—Google likes relevant links between pages.

- **Writing longer pieces of content**
  Longer articles tend to rank better than shorter ones. Articles over 2,000 words seem to do best.

- **Optimizing your website's loading speed**
  Another very important aspect that can improve your website ranking is its speed, or loading time. This is especially important because many visitors will come to your site using a mobile phone, and it tends to take longer to load on mobile phones. Free WordPress plugins, such as Ewww Image Optimizer and Autoptimize, can be installed to increase your site speed.

These are the SEO elements you have the most control over—the *on-site* SEO. To help optimize your website pages for search engines, I recommend you install the Yoast SEO plugin.

We won't spend a lot of time talking about *off-site* SEO practices. However, it's worth mentioning one very important factor (if not *the* most important) for Google to determine which sites rank highly in the results: "backlinking." Backlinking is when another website links to yours—genuinely. You don't want to pay to get backlinks, nor do you want links from low-quality websites.

In the past, website owners would put their domain and web page links into several other websites—not always of good quality—just to get links back to their site and improve their ranking. Today, this practice is no longer really effective.

Even though any genuine links from other sites will help you rank higher in the search engines, Google puts more importance on links from highly authoritative sites, with the highest being *.edu* and *.gov* sites. To get authoritative sites to link to yours, you must provide incredible value that others will consider worth mentioning.

There is so much to cover with SEO; this was only a short overview to help you understand the role it can play in driving traffic to your site. SEO should be seen as a long-term approach to generating traffic, but it's worth optimizing your on-site elements from the start to help you eventually be found organically through search engines.

12. Paid Search Results (SEM)

Organic results and paid results (sponsored links) both appear in the search engine results.

The first results at the top of the page are of the sponsored variety, while the others are organic (the ones we referred to in the last section about SEO). It is entirely possible to pay a given search engine to appear on the first page results. That's what we call search engine marketing (SEM).

Google's system for sponsored results is called *Google AdWords*. It's a bidding system where companies bid on keywords to get the chance to be shown in the paid results at the top, or on the right-side column, of the first page. Thus, the price for this type of advertising depends on the bids placed by other companies to appear for the same keyword. Some keywords are more competitive than others, and are therefore more expensive to bid on.

Even if 95% of all clicks come from organic result links, it's usually difficult to organically appear within the results of the first page, so it can be interesting to use Google AdWords to increase visibility.

However, before you venture into SEM, I recommend that you learn the system well in order to optimize your return on investment, or the revenue generated from sales versus what you'll end up paying to Google. For example, since you're charged each time your link is clicked on, it's very important that the page where visitors are sent after clicking is a good sales page to increase the conversion of visitors into buyers.

SEM can be very pricey, so make sure you understand very well how to choose your keywords before launching a campaign with Google AdWords. Read a book or even take a short course on the topic. It'll save you money in the long run!

Don't Forget Your Main Goal

Always remember your main goal when driving traffic to your website: **building your email list.**

You should be sending traffic to a page with the best chances of converting visitors into subscribers on your email list—a squeeze page. This could increase the conversion into subscribers by up to 10 times.

Whether you publish an article on a popular blog, are interviewed in a podcast, or promote yourself on social media, remember your main objective and choose to send people to a squeeze page designed for this purpose, rather than linking to your homepage or an article on your site.

Network with Influential People

Building relationships with people in your field is also very important to grow your business. These relationships can be even stronger if you meet in person. There are several ways and occasions to meet influential people: through mentorship, by being part of a mastermind group, and by attending live events, such as conferences, seminars and Meetup events.

Mentorship

Everyone could benefit from access to a more knowledgeable person for advice, feedback and guidance. Having the guidance of a mentor can prevent many mistakes from being made by the mentee (you) and provide shortcuts through the process of building your business.

The main difficulty is actually *finding* a mentor. A mentor is someone who has already achieved what you aim for, and is therefore usually a very busy person. Once you've connected with someone who agrees to provide you with advice and guidance, note that s/he might not have the time to meet with you every week for three hours. However, a good mentor should agree to exchange emails and phone calls, once in a while, to answer some important questions that you may have regarding your business.

How can you find such a person? Start by making a list of a few individuals who have achieved what you're aiming for. Choose the ones that aren't the top of their field—thus the busiest—but who are knowledgeable enough to help you. Do some research on them, on the projects they have worked on, the causes they support, etc. It's best to find a mentor that shares the same values as you. Then, get in touch through email. You could also browse LinkedIn profiles or ask someone in a LinkedIn group of which you are a member. An even better way would be to connect with people at live events, especially Meetup events.

If you can't find a "personal" mentor—one that will guide you one-on-one—learn from experts by other means. Listen to podcasts, take online courses, and read books and blogs. Thanks to the Internet, you have access to an ocean of information—take advantage of it. As we said, entrepreneurs must love learning.

Mastermind Groups

A mastermind group is a small group of people—ideally three to five—in the same field who meet on a regular basis to talk about their projects, give and get advice and feedback, and hold each other accountable.

This is an excellent way to meet like-minded people and build long-term relationships, as well as to get support in building and growing your business. Think of it as an opportunity to exchange information, experience, and expertise, as well as to create partnerships. I believe this is even more crucial for online entrepreneurs. As it isn't a very common field (yet), it's often difficult to get the support and understanding we need from our friends and relatives.

Perhaps you're wondering how to find people to form a mastermind group? First, note that you'll want to connect with people who are serious and ready to meet regularly. It's not always easy to find! Therefore, look for people at your level, or who are a little more advanced than you, since they will help you to progress faster. You can find potential members through Facebook groups, the Meetup groups in your city, or when attending workshops.

While it's probably better to meet in person, if the members of your mastermind group are located in different cities, you can hold the sessions online using a platform like Google Hangouts.

Events

There are plenty of live events, conferences, and seminars related to online business. Here are just a few:

- New Media Expo and Blog World (*BlogWorld.com*)
- TNW Conference (*TheNextWeb.com*)
- Social Media Marketing World (*SocialMediaExaminer.com*)
- Digital Summit Phoenix (*DigitalSummitPhoenix.com*)
- Content Marketing World (*ContentMarketingWorld.com*)
- Podcast Movement (*PodcastMovement.com*)

These are only a few examples. You can find many other events and some that are more specific to your topic and niche in a simple Google search. There are conferences for food bloggers, eCommerce businesses, authorpreneurs, etc.

Other less formal events are also great opportunities to build relationships. A good example is World Domination Summit (*WorldDominationSummit.com*), where you can attend workshops and participate in several activities. You could even become a volunteer at a TedX event in your city to meet inspiring people.

MeetUp.com

Meetup events are a great and easy way to meet and connect with people in your industry. Members of a group have varying levels of expertise. You could find a mentor, form a mastermind group with other members, create partnerships, and get access to several other opportunities.

Just as an example, I'm part of several Meetup groups related to online business and marketing in my city. Once, the founders of one of these groups announced that they were looking for guest writers for their blog. It was a great opportunity for members to get more exposure and drive traffic to their website.

Through Meetup events, I've also found a mentor, someone I meet a couple of times each month for coffee to get advice and guidance. I've also formed a mastermind group. If you can't find a group related to your field, don't be afraid to create one!

What to Remember About Getting Traffic

1) To drive quality traffic to your website, you must know who your ideal customers are and expose yourself where they already hang out.

2) To make sure visitors will want to come back to your site, you must have useful information and provide high-quality content that's interesting to them.

3) At the beginning, you'll want to spend more time promoting your content than creating it.

4) Trying to be everywhere will be overwhelming and is ultimately ineffective. Choose just a few of these methods to drive visitors to your site:

- Guest posting on popular blogs
- Accepting guest writers on your website
- Being interviewed on podcasts
- Interviewing experts in your field
- Hosting webinars
- Having a presence and building a community on social media
- Creating SlideShare presentations
- Answering questions on forums
- Posting on bookmarking sites
- Writing an eBook and publishing it in the Amazon Kindle store
- Optimizing your website for search engines (SEO)
- Using search engine advertising (Google AdWords) to appear in the paid search results (SEM)

5) Guest posting and publishing on Amazon are probably the two most effective tactics to drive traffic to your website.

6) Building relationships with people in your field is crucial to growing your business. You can meet people by:
- Forming a mastermind group
- Finding a mentor
- Attending live events
- Becoming a member of Meetup groups

Take Action

(Suggested time for the exercise: One week)

1) Determine the two social media platforms where you have the best chance of connecting with your target audience.

- o   Learn how to use the platform in depth through YouTube tutorials or *Udemy.com* or *SkillShare.com* courses.

2) Choose one tactic other than social media to drive traffic to your website.

This can be interacting on forums, answering questions on Quora, writing a book, creating SlideShare presentations, etc.

3) Make a list of websites and blogs where you could eventually guest post.

- o   Make sure they accept guest writers
- o   Read several posts and the comments people have left
- o   Comment and share the bloggers' content

4) Install the Yoast SEO plugin to increase your website's optimization for search engines (SEO).

5) Make a list of live events in your industry.

6) Become a member of Meetup groups related to your topic, or create a new one.

7) Form a mastermind group.

8) Make a list of potential mentors and contact them.

CHAPTER 9

STARTING TO GENERATE REVENUE

At first, you might have thought that creating and selling products would be the most challenging aspect of an online business, but don't worry... it's not.

You've already done most of the work by finding a topic and a niche, defining your audience, creating your ideal customer's avatar, generating traffic to your website and building an email list. *That* was the hardest part of building your business. Afterwards, creating and selling products or services should be quite easy... at least it is in the digital world.

The type of products or services you can offer is almost unlimited. We'll cover a few of the most important ones and we'll mention a few resources to help you in the process.

Freelancing

Freelancers are self-employed individuals who sell work or services by the hour or by job completion, rather than working on a regular salary basis for one employer.

As a freelancer, you can offer your services through your own website or through marketplace platforms, such as:

- *Upwork.com*
- *Freelancer.com*
- *Guru.com*
- *Freelance.com*
- *WeWorkRemotely.com*

As a freelancer, you can bid on the jobs posted on the site or be directly contacted for a specific project. Usually, the intermediary service—the freelancing platform—gets a percentage of the total revenue generated for a job.

You can also offer your services through your personal website, but there needs to be more promotional effort made. In this case, all of the tactics mentioned in the preceding chapter about driving traffic to your site can be used to promote your freelancing services.

LinkedIn, for example, can be very useful. On LinkedIn, you can request former clients to recommend you. Recommendations are social proof of your skills and expertise. Plus, by using accurate keywords in your profile to describe your skill sets, you'll enable new potential clients to find you.

If you manage to build a team of complementary talents, you could take on more complex projects and share the revenues with your team members. You could also delegate some parts of a project by hiring people , or even delegate the whole process and act as a project manager. You can find team members through freelancing marketplaces or within Facebook and LinkedIn groups.

Finally, creating and selling online courses or eBooks that teach elements related to your field of expertise could add new—and more passive—income streams to your freelancing revenue. A great example is Nathan Barry (*NathanbBarry.com*), a former freelancer who ended up generating a considerable income selling eBooks about web application design.

If you would like to take your freelancing business to the next level, I recommend taking Seth Godin's marketing and business course for freelancers, available on *Udemy.com*. Seth is one of today's most respected marketers, and his three-hour course is highly rated.

Online Coaching or Consulting

Online coaching or consulting can be offered in addition to in-person services.

It primarily enables the consultant to work with clients located remotely and to work from home or anywhere else. It basically eliminates the distance barrier with potential clients. Sessions can be conducted through Skype, Google Hangouts or *ooVoo.com*, among other services.

Some great ways to promote your coaching and consulting service include guest posting on other blogs, self-publishing eBooks on Amazon Kindle, and hosting webinars.

By tackling a specific problem expressed within your niche market and providing some elements of a solution, you can promote your services as a more in-depth solution at the end of a webinar. You'll easily find the most urgent pain or desires of your target audience by looking at forums related to your topic.

Depending on your industry, there are also intermediary platforms, or directories, where you can offer your consulting services, such as:

- *Clarity.fm*: Business consulting
- *Quantifye.co*: Business consulting
- *LifeCoachOnDemand.com*: Life coaching

Selling Other People's Products (Affiliate Marketing)

You can make a commission on others' products that you sell when you're enrolled in their affiliate program.

To do this, you promote their products using an affiliate link provided by the advertiser. This link is only for you to use and will tell the advertiser that *you* made the sale. After clicking on the link, the visitor will be sent to the product's sales page. If the product is then purchased, you'll get a commission.

You should only recommend excellent products that will be useful to your audience. It is *your* responsibility to ensure that your product is of great quality. Promote products from people you know and/or have personally used and really liked. Recommending a bad product, or one that wouldn't be useful to your audience, would harm the trust they have in you. This hard-to-build trust is crucial to the relationship you have with your audience.

If there's a product you would like to sell to your audience, you can contact the company directly and ask to become a partner. Another way to find affiliate products is by searching on intermediary platforms that connect advertisers and publishers, such as:

- *ClickBank.com*
- *JvZoo.com*
- *cj.com*
- *Amazon.com (affiliate-program.amazon.com)*

Simply create an account, browse products, and select the ones your audience could greatly benefit from.

Don't forget that you must let people know when a product you are recommending is an affiliate. You could simply say "here is my affiliate link for this product" and tell them that buying from this link helps you, at no extra cost to them. For more detailed information about partnership disclosure, I invite you to read the FTC guidelines.

Creating and Selling Your Own Products

There is a big difference between selling physical products online and selling digital products. The costs associated with production, stocking and delivery are basically non-existent for digital products, but can be considerable for physical ones.

Types of Digital Products

As we mentioned when we discussed the different online business models in Chapter 1, the most profitable model is usually creating and selling your own digital products.

Once you have defined your niche market and found your audience's pain and desires, you are well equipped to design the best product to solve this pain. What you have to choose at that point is the format you'll use to present a solution.

The most common formats are courses, eBooks, online live events (webinars), membership sites, audio tracks, software and digital magazines.

1. Online Courses and Training

If you have knowledge and information that could be useful to others, you should consider packaging it into an online course. It could be produced in a video, audio, or written format, or even a combination of them. A course should teach the audience how to achieve a specific objective. Courses can be created around almost any topic, as long as there are enough people interested in learning what you intend to teach.

If you already have an email list of a few hundred or more engaged subscribers, it would be advantageous to sell your course through your own website, or to host it on a platform such as

Teachable.com, which facilitates the process of building the course and delivering the content to your audience. You could also allow others to promote the course for you by becoming affiliates.

If you don't have an audience yet, but have knowledge to share, you could offer your digital course through intermediary platforms, such as *Udemy.com*, *SkillShare.com* and *Lynda.com*. The profit margin will be lower since the intermediary will take a percentage, but it can be a great way to start, since you'll have access to the platform's audience.

If the creation of an online video course intimidates you, know that there are many resources available to help you. *Udemy.com* offers a free class for aspiring instructors (*Teach.Udemy.com*) that explains the process of creating a course, including the technical and marketing aspects. You can also become a member of their Facebook group for instructors, where you can ask questions to a supportive community of online teachers. Even if you decide to sell your course on your own website, those free Udemy resources can be very helpful.

There are also plugins you can install on your WordPress website that facilitate the task of creating and delivering a course. Some of these plugins are:

- *ZippyCourses*
- *TeachPress*
- *Sensei*
- *LearnDash*

To build your course efficiently, break the information down into chunks and place it in a logical sequence to ensure a good understanding by the audience.

Start by giving an overview of the learning process, introducing the problem you propose to solve, as well as the solution offered, along with the benefits associated. Then, present the process, step-by-step, from the current problematic situation to achieving the end result benefits.

2. eBooks

Writing and self-publishing an eBook can not only help you gain more authority in your field, facilitate connections with influencers, and increase your reach and exposure, but it can also generate a significant income.

Until you have collected a considerable amount of email subscribers to your list, you'll probably want to take advantage of the Amazon Kindle self-publishing platform. This may surprise you, but there are individuals making a very good living writing and self-publishing eBooks. Some successful authorpreneurs, like Steve Scott (*DevelopGoodHabits.com*) and Chandler Bolt (co-author of *The Productive Person*), just to name two, have managed to build a highly profitable business around self-publishing books on Amazon.

However, once you've grown an email list of over 1,000 engaged subscribers, it becomes even more interesting, since you then have an audience to sell your eBooks to directly. You don't have to share the revenue with an intermediary and can start making a more substantial income from your books.

Once again, if you're interested in publishing in the Amazon Kindle store, I highly recommend that you listen to Steve Scott's podcast *Self-Publishing Questions* on iTunes.

3. Webinars and Live Events

We've mentioned webinars as a way to promote and drive traffic to your website, but they can also take the form of paid online events. As the webinar organizer or host, you simply share information and knowledge that's useful for an audience that pays to receive it.

You can be the one delivering the content, or you can find an expert to do so—for the latter, you would simply share the revenues with the expert, or pay him/her a fixed fee up front.

Webinars can also be a great way to collect information about your audience. While presenting the content, attendees will ask questions, which can help you identify their main difficulties and desires. This is very valuable information that you can use to create another live event, or even a course or an eBook to sell. You could also decide to host a free webinar and use the occasion to sell another product.

Larger live events, such as *Social Media Success Summit*, take considerably more work to organize. They imply continuous work, and thus aren't considered a passive income unless you sell the replay. However, if you manage to generate sufficient revenues from an event, it could be well worth it to put one in place.

If you would like to learn how to create and present webinars, John Lee Dumas *(Entrepreneur On Fire podcast)* offers a free 10-day webinar course.

Finally, if you need to review the tactics to promote your webinar or other live events and gain attendees, I invite you to go back to Chapter 8 and read the part about hosting webinars in the traffic sources section.

4. Membership Sites

On membership sites, members pay a recurring fee to have access to content—information, knowledge and advice—that you provide. The fee is usually monthly, but could be annually, bi-annually, or on any other basis you think is most suitable to the topic of your site.

This business model is especially suitable for topics that require a long period of study. For example, guitar classes could be a good fit for a membership site, since it takes some time for a person to progress from a beginner to an expert level. The learning process can take several months, from learning the fundamental basics of guitar playing to gaining the capacity to play more complex melodies.

With a membership site, you'll have to deliver content on a regular basis to justify the recurring fee. It would be a good idea to have several pieces of content, enough for the first month or two, ready by the time you launch your site.

To create a membership platform, you can simply install a plugin on your WordPress site that will enable you to enroll and manage members and deliver content. A good plugin that I recommend is *Wishlist.com*.

Another element that is often used to justify the recurring fee of a membership site is access to a community of like-minded members. In that case, a forum can be set up to facilitate communication between members. There are also plugins for forums that you can install on your website, in addition to the membership one, such as *BbPress.org* and *BuddyPress.org*.

5. Audio

Audio products may include audiobooks, paid podcasts, music, meditation tracks, etc. They can be sold and downloaded directly from your website or through platforms like iTunes, *Audible.com*, *SongCastMusic.com* and *Gumroad.com*, among others. The sound quality for this format is crucial, so make sure that you use a good microphone and reduce ambient sound as much as possible.

6. Software Products

Software products include WordPress plugins, and smartphone and web applications. They have the potential to generate high and passive revenues. The downside associated with this business model is usually the high production cost and the probable necessity to occasionally update the product. However, there are almost no costs to reproduce the software once it's created.

If this is a model that interests you, there is a highly respected program founded by Dane Maxwell and Andy Drish called *The Foundation*. This program teaches aspiring entrepreneurs to build a software business without the need to have any programming skills. The technical aspects are outsourced, since the program is directed towards identifying a problem in a market and finding a solution.

7. Digital Magazines

With the rise of the popularity of mobile devices, digital magazines are another interesting product to create. Plus, there are now software solutions that make the magazines very easy to build. Two such software products are:

- *Magcast.co*
- *InHouseDigitalPublishing.com*

To generate revenue, you can charge a subscription fee and sell advertising space to other businesses. An example of a successful digital magazine is *Foundrmag.com*, launched in 2013.

The Concept of a Minimum Viable Product

Perhaps you've heard of the concept of a "lean startup." It's a strategy used to reduce market risks by releasing products in their minimum viable form, and then observing the market response.

The product is first created based on a hypothesis—the hypothesis that the market needs it. If the product generates enough sales to be profitable, the hypothesis is confirmed. Thus, investing in the creation of a more complete—and more expensive to produce—version of the product is justified. This process enables businesses to validate their idea before investing a lot of time and money into its development. It basically allows them to get the highest return on investment versus risks.

When you plan on creating a product, it is a good idea to take the lean startup approach. Start by making a "minimum viable" version of the product, introduce it to your niche market, and observe the response before spending time, money, and effort on a more complex project.

For example, if you're planning to write a 200-page eBook, why not begin by writing a 30-page, less detailed version of it? Or try a couple of blog posts on the same topic, to publish on your website or someone else's, and observe if it triggers engagement?

Releasing an initial basic version of a product is also a very common practice in the software industry. Based on the users' feedback, adjustments are made and the software is improved to better satisfy the users' needs.

For online courses, you could use a platform such as *Udemy.com* to release a shorter, less complex version of a course you would like to create, and see what the response is.

I would also recommend the book *Will It Fly?* by Pat Flynn, which could help you validate your business or product idea.

Pre-selling the Product

Some entrepreneurs will choose to pre-sell their product before it's even created to make sure there will be buyers. They simply announce the product, say that it will be available on date X, and allow people to pre-order it. If there are buyers, the entrepreneur will immediately begin production.

If you decide to use this strategy, make sure that you've given yourself enough time to create the product when setting the launch date. You should have a plan and everything to start building it on hand.

Using Webinars for Product Validation

Before creating a product, you could prepare a webinar on the same topic and see if there are people interested in attending. If you get a few attendees, it's a good sign that there are people willing to learn about the subject and that there could potentially be buyers for a paid product. Webinars can also be an opportunity to pre-sell your product.

Asking People Why They Didn't Buy

If you've offered a product to your email subscribers that you thought they could benefit from, but they didn't buy, don't be shy; send them an email asking *why* they didn't buy. It'll give you very valuable information about what went wrong. Was it the product's features themselves? Or were the benefits of the product misunderstood? Asking your audience why they didn't buy the product will help you improve your offer and ensure that it will be better received next time.

Don't Wait Too Long Before Selling Something

One mistake many entrepreneurs make when they are just starting out is waiting too long before offering a paid product. Often, they wait out of fear of a negative response from their audience. *"Will they get mad at me because I'm selling something?"*

Well, there will always be some individuals who complain, and yes, some will react negatively to the offer of a paid product. Does it matter? It shouldn't. The audience members who are complaining are *not* your ideal customers, and you *do not* want them as part of your audience. Let them be, and let them go. You can't possibly please everyone, so don't waste your energy in attempting to do so.

By getting your audience accustomed to being offered paid products or services early, you'll diminish the risk of a negative response later, as it won't take them by surprise. As mentioned in a previous chapter, within the first few emails of the series you send to new subscribers, you could include an offer as simple as a book recommendation for which you are an affiliate (for example, through an Amazon affiliate program).

What to Remember About Generating Revenue

1) The main ways to generate revenues online are:
- Freelancing
- Online consulting or coaching
- Affiliate marketing
- Creating and selling physical products
- Creating and selling digital products

2) Creating and selling digital products is usually what generates the highest revenues. There are several formats of digital products:
- eBooks
- Courses and training
- Webinars
- Membership sites
- Audio tracks
- Software products
- Digital magazines

3) Before plunging into the creation of a complex product that's costly to create, you should first test your idea by launching a basic version and observing the market's response to it. This strategy is called creating a "minimum viable product."

4) To lower the risks as much as possible, you could also pre-sell your product, even before it has been created.

5) Webinars can be used for idea validation. If people attend a webinar (free or paid) to learn about a specific topic, you can make the hypothesis that there will potentially be customers for a paid product on the same topic.

6) When you don't get the results you were wishing for from a product launch—your product didn't sell well—a good idea is to send an email to your audience members asking them *why* they didn't buy. This can give you valuable information to help you achieve better results in the future.

Take Action

(Suggested time to allow for the exercise: 3 hours)

1) According to your situation (audience, topic, expertise), pick a method of generating revenues and explore it thoroughly. Take the time to research and understand the method you have selected. Get this important information through podcasts, online courses and other resources.

2) If you plan on creating your own product, think of a minimum viable version of it to use to validate your idea before investing a lot of time and money into the creation of a complex version.

CHAPTER 10

SETTING A PRICE FOR YOUR PRODUCT

How much should you sell your product for?

The price is a characteristic of your product. It's part of its branding and also of its market positioning—its place in the market compared to other similar offers (competitors).

Pricing is therefore an important element to consider when you build your business, not only as a mean of generating revenues, but also as an element that impacts how your product will be perceived by potential consumers.

Pricing is often an element of discomfort among new entrepreneurs. Likely caused by a lack of experience and thus confidence, putting a price on a new product or service can make many new business owners nervous.

Many entrepreneurs don't know how much to charge and aren't sure of the value of the new product. They might also fear the market's reaction. Will they think the price is too high? What if they leave a comment on the web saying, "It certainly wasn't worth the cost!"?

However, remember the definition of a business: getting remunerated for the value you bring to a market. There shouldn't be any shame in getting paid for providing value.

Pricing Is (First) a Psychological Thing

If you keep your price low because of a lack of confidence in your own product, it will show. The price of a product is often associated with its (perceived) quality. If you think that by offering your product at a very low price, you'll avoid potential complaints and will navigate in a safer zone, don't be so sure.

Before we get into more detail, I would like to share a little story.

A short time ago, I was part of a mastermind group of web entrepreneurs and bloggers. At the first meeting, we all introduced ourselves. One member was a life coach. He introduced himself and explained what he was doing, with obvious confidence:

"Come to see me once, and you will feel aligned and get the ability to be laser-focused on what you are meant to achieve in life. Just one session with me will change your life." Wow. Even I wanted to book an appointment with him right away. His speech was very convincing. Then, we asked him how much he was charging per session. I expected $1,000. He could have said $1,500, and it would have seemed justified. However, he said $250, for one hour of his time. What do you think happened in my mind? Did I think "What a bargain!"?

Well, not exactly. It made me doubt his promise and the result he was selling. In just a one-hour session with him, my life would be changed, for only $250? Something felt wrong about that. That "something" was the cost of his service. It was simply too low, and that low price diminished the perceived quality of his offer.

Do you see how pricing is primarily a psychological thing?

Does this mean it's better to sell your offerings at a higher price just to increase the perceived value? Well, no… but the displayed price should be in accordance with the benefit you are promising.

Pricing is also often related to status. Some people will always buy the most expensive watches and shoes because they want their "social status" to show in their clothing and accessories.

Your chosen positioning strategy in the market—your product compared to your competitors'—should also have an influence when determining the price, as it's one element that consumers will use to evaluate your offer.

Whatever price you are willing to let your product sell for, there should be a good reason to back it up. A lower price isn't necessarily a bad thing, as long as you justify it. The same is true for a higher price.

How to Define the Price of Your Product

What is the Purpose of Your Product?

The first question to answer is: "Why are you offering this product in the first place?"

Is it to:

- o Gain credibility? (Often the case in publishing a book or creating a blog)
- o Get more email subscribers to your website?
- o Generate revenue?

Why does the purpose of your product matter? If you hope to collect leads (email subscribers), then you have a reason to give your product away or at a lower price, since the emails alone have a high value. In this case, a low price won't diminish your product's perceived value. It will be justified, and even advantageous, since you want to get as many quality visitors to subscribe to your list as possible.

If you wish to gain credibility, then money isn't the main goal, either. You shouldn't settle for a very low or very high price, but more for something in the middle. However, if you want to generate revenue, then yes, you should aim for a higher price.

What's the Paying Capacity of Your Target Market?

If you've done some research into your avatar's (ideal customer's) profile, you should have an idea about its income, its discretionary budget, and its willingness to pay for the type of product you are offering.

What *could* your audience pay for your product?

If your target market is single parents on benefits or college students, and you're selling a giant home cinema screen, there's a good chance that this market, even if interested in your offer, won't have the ability to pay for it.

Ask yourself: "Can they pay?"

This is actually an important aspect to consider when deciding on a niche. Ideally, you want to serve a market that has discretionary income to spend on non-essential goods.

What is the Market's Reference Price?

What's the price for similar options offered in the market? At what price are your competitors selling comparable products?

That should also be a good indicator. Look at your competitors' product characteristics and related pricing. Compare the characteristics of their offer versus yours. Then, think of the position in the market that you would like to occupy. Are you a low-cost, average, or high-end option?

Cover Your Costs

What is your fixed cost, or the cost you pay independently of how many items you create? What are your variable costs, or the cost per product created?

For example, if you write a book, your fixed cost will include the production of your book, including the writing time, the cover illustration, the editing, and proofreading. The variable cost will include the printing and distribution fees per book.

Unless you've decided to give your product away for free, you'll want to cover both your fixed and variable costs. If the purpose of creating your product is to generate revenue, then you may want to sell it for at least three times its variable cost of production. On the other hand, if the purpose is to generate leads (subscribers), then you might not need to cover your costs, since it will be considered more as an investment.

What's the Perceived Value of the Benefit Your Customers Will Gain After Consuming Your Product?

How beneficial is the end result provided by your offer to your target market? What's the perceived value of that benefit?

For example, how much would a person who wants to lose ten pounds to look great before the summer be willing to pay for a weight loss program? What about a woman who wants to fit into her wedding dress? Or a man who needs to lower his cholesterol to avoid imminent health problems?

Your target market will be more or less sensitive to price depending on the importance of overcoming the "pain" as well as its urgency.

Also, what will it take for your customers to overcome the "pain"? If you're offering a weight loss program that guarantees good results within two months by following an exercise and healthy cooking plan, how much would the average person who wants to lose weight quickly be ready to pay? How much would that same person be willing to pay for a simple, natural pill that guarantees the same results? Probably more than the exercise plan, as the effort required for achieving the end result is smaller.

The benefits to be gained by using the product, and the effort required, should be considered when deciding on the product's price.

The Mattress Method

Marie Forleo, business coach and entrepreneur, has a great way of explaining the perceived value of a product: the Mattress Method. Can you translate the value of your product into real-life currency, like time, money, love, and health?

She gives an example of the day she went shopping for a new mattress. The mattress she was looking at was more expensive than other types offered on the market, but the salesman reminded her that:

- You spend one-third of your time in bed
- Good sleep improves your productivity, health, and good looks

Essentially, the salesman told her that good sleep contributed in making her richer, healthier, and prettier. These are the tangible benefits of the product in real-life currency. What is the perceived value of the benefits your customers will gain after purchasing your product?

Your Portfolio of Products

You should offer multiple levels of products or services.

For example, if you have an eBook selling for $19, an online course at $79, and a one-hour consultation at $250, you have a portfolio of three products. Offering multiple levels of products gives people a price reference point.

In the example above, if you only sell an eBook and an online course, the online course may be perceived by consumers as too expensive, but when you add a pricier item—the $250 consultation—to the portfolio, it makes the middle offer seem more affordable. It's psychological. Most people will opt for the middle option.

Another reason to consider a product portfolio might surprise you: some people will only want the high-end option. If you don't offer a high-end option or a more expensive product, they will buy one elsewhere.

In the book *80/20 Sales and Marketing*, Perry Marshall explains that there will always be people willing to buy a very expensive offer. He gives the example of Starbucks. Starbucks sells cups of regular filter coffee for $2.50. You can also buy a complete breakfast for about $12, including a soy latte, biscotti, and a fruit salad. But have you noticed the espresso machine also available for sale? Of course, not many customers will buy the $400 espresso machine, but a few will. If Starbucks didn't offer an espresso machine, the customer who wanted to buy one would get it from somewhere else. Starbucks would lose a sale for not offering the product.

Do you have a high-end product to offer? If not, can you create one? Not only will offering one make your other, lower cost products look more affordable to your customers' eyes, but not offering one will most likely cause you to lose potential sales.

The bottom line is to offer multiple levels of products or services. It helps people to make a purchase decision when they can compare products and prices.

Discounts Are Dangerous

As a general rule, it's better to avoid offering discounts.

Discounted rates are addictive. When people see your product offered at a discount, they'll have a harder time buying it at the regular price later. They may expect further discounts and wait for one before buying.

Plus, discounting can evoke confusion towards the perceived quality of the product you are offering. If it's sold for less, does that mean it's worth less than what it was previously offered for?

The question is: What should you do instead?

A better approach is to add extra value for a limited time. In the context of a launch, this may include adding another item to the original offer as a bonus.

For example, if you're selling an online course on outdoor photography, you could offer a free eBook on how to take great sunrise and sunset shots to the first 10 buyers.

If your product is a book, you could offer the audio version at no extra fee, for a limited number of copies sold or for a limited time.

It's a bargain for your audience without diminishing the perceived value of your main product or accustoming consumers to discounted prices. Note that the bonus item should be relevant to the main product and, ideally, should complement it.

If You Really Want to Offer a Discount

In this case, be sure to justify the discount. Give a reason for why you are offering it.

Is it for clearance? Is it your organization's 10th anniversary, so you'll happily give away a discount to celebrate? Or are you giving a special discounted offer to your most loyal customers to thank them?

Whatever the reason, mention it. Let people know that this is for a special occasion to make sure they won't expect frequent discounts in the future.

All-inclusive resorts in regions near the tropics offer discounted rates during the northern hemisphere summer, because fewer people are buying their vacation products during that period. That's justified. They have a reason to lower the price, as the low season means less occupancy. These resorts could do even better—they could upgrade their regular offer. Instead of discounting the price of a room, they could offer dining vouchers or free excursions during the low season.

Don't Worry About People Complaining About Your Product's Price

Ramit Sethi, author of *I Will Teach You To Be Rich*, has been asked many times to talk about pricing on different podcasts and live shows, such as *The Smart Passive Income* or *Chase Jarvis Live*.

He admitted to having had trouble charging for his products at the beginning. He feared his audience's reaction, even if his first product was a five-dollar eBook! And yes, some members of his audience *did* complain.

"How dare you charge us for your content?!"

Ramit had been delivering valuable information, for free, for about two years before selling his $5 eBook.

Well, what does this teach us? It tells us that there will always be those who complain!

Fortunately, these complainers usually only constitute a very small percentage of an audience, and they aren't part of an audience that you *want* to serve. They don't represent your ideal customer. Ramit's audience members who complained about the $5 eBook, even after they had happily consumed two years of valuable free content, weren't worthy of his attention.

The bottom line is that there will always be unhappy people, and that's okay. Live with it, and stop being scared of putting a price on your product.

That said, if the complaints you're getting with regards to your product's price are generalized, maybe you *did* do something wrong. In that case, listen to the **constructive** negative feedback, and, if possible, modify your price accordingly.

What to Remember About Pricing

1) Pricing is part of branding and positioning.

2) Pricing is very psychological:
    - It's often associated with quality.
    - It can also be related to status.

3) To determine your product's price, there are some elements to consider:
    - The purpose of your product
    - The paying capacity of your target market (niche)
    - The market's reference price (other similar options offered on the market)
    - The perceived value of the solution or benefit your product provides

4) It's better to offer multiple levels of products in order to have a portfolio of products of different value and at different prices.

5) Instead of discounting your product, offer bonus items for a limited number of purchases or for a limited time to add extra value. This way, it won't diminish the perceived value of the original offer, and it will avoid accustoming your customers to discounted rates.

Take Action

(Suggested time to allow for the exercise: 1.5 hours)

1) Answer the following questions:

- What is the purpose of your product?
  Is it to generate revenue, to gain credibility in your field, to get email subscribers, or another reason?

- What's the average income and discretionary income (part of the income left for unessential goods purchases) of your target audience?
  Do they have the capacity to buy your product at a certain price?

- At what price are your competitors selling similar products, and what are the characteristics of their offer? Compare their products with yours. Also, state what your position in the market is (low-cost, average, or high-end).

- How important and urgent is it to solve the "pain" (the problem or the desire) of your target market?
  What value do the benefits of your product have in your market's eyes?

2) Create a portfolio of products.

Determine three products or services of different value and in different price ranges that you could offer to create a portfolio (multiple levels of products).

3) Identify potential bonus items.

Identify a few bonus items relevant to your main products that you could offer in a bundle to add extra value to your original offer (for a limited time, or a limited amount of purchases, on special occasions).

CHAPTER 11

CONVINCING POTENTIAL CUSTOMERS

There are two main elements that play a huge role in convincing potential customers to consider your offer. One is the trust they have in you as a person, and the other is the confidence they have that the product will solve their problem.

There is an emphasis on the word *trust.* When we tackle persuasion techniques in this section, don't get me wrong—I'm not talking about manipulating your audience!

You (hopefully) want to build honest and lasting relationships with your buyers. You *do* have a genuine desire to serve your market and help them solve their problem, and sincerely believe that your product or service has the capacity to solve it, right? In that case, you simply have to find the best way to tell them.

Persuasion Techniques

Let's dive right into persuasion techniques. Persuasion is often synonymous with the power of influence, and can even be associated with seduction and manipulation.

In the context of selling your product or service, however, it's more about convincing your potential customers of your offer's real capacity to solve their problem. This is a very important step that can determine how many sales you'll make.

If you genuinely believe in the value of your product and in the positive impact it will have on your target market, you should definitely be equipped to share its benefits with potential customers.

The Six Laws of Persuasion

It's almost impossible to tackle the theme of persuasion without quoting the psychology and marketing expert, Dr. Robert Cialdini. His field research on the topic resulted in the 1984 bestselling book, titled *Influence: The Psychology of Persuasion.*

Cialdini's research led to the finding of six main elements that contribute to persuading others.

These factors can and should be used on your website, mainly on your product sales page, and even on your About page.

Here are the six elements:

1. Reciprocation

You probably have a friend who once paid for the two beers you had at the bar, even though it wasn't your birthday or any other special occasion. Perhaps it surprised you, and you felt a mixture of gratitude and discomfort. Maybe you told yourself—or even your friend—that next time, drinks would be on you.

The law of reciprocation stipulates that when someone does us a favor, we feel the obligation to return it. Until we do so, we feel a kind of discomfort—we *owe* something.

You've probably heard marketers say that you should give tons of value to your audience before asking for anything. Once you've given your audience value (free content, video courses, eBooks, blog posts, etc.), they will most likely be willing to buy your paid product in the future. Not only will they trust you, but they might also feel the need to reciprocate and give back to you.

Bottom line: Give and you shall receive.

2. Credibility

Have you ever consulted a therapist or a specialist? While alone in the room waiting for the therapist to enter, didn't you take a quick glance at the walls, looking for credentials? And didn't you feel somehow relieved when you saw them?

Credibility is about demonstrating your expertise on a topic. It's about showing your competence to solve your audience's problem.

Do you have a diploma? Display it. Wrote a book on the topic? Add a link to it. Have worked many years in the field? Explain that in your bio.

If you have good knowledge on a topic, years of practice in the field, or any other type of authority, it'll be easier to convince people that you can help them solve their problem.

If you've personally gone through the same undesirable situation in the past and have managed to successfully resolve the issue, you can also be considered knowledgeable in the field. If you've acquired a title like a PhD, for example, mention it. It will enhance your authority.

Show your credentials, diplomas, experience, and authority title. It will make people more confident that you are the best person to help them.

3. Commitment and Consistency

If you told your mother that you would drive her to the airport, but the day before her departure, told her that you wouldn't be able to follow through on your commitment, you would probably feel guilty.

When we commit to doing something, we naturally feel obligated to keep our word, or we feel at fault.

As Cialdini says, "We're more likely to do something after we've agreed to it verbally or in writing." For example, it's been shown that when therapists let their clients write the date of their next appointment on the card themselves, fewer no-shows are registered.

We also prefer to follow pre-existing attitudes, values, and actions. If we act in a way that contradicts our previous behaviors, we'll most likely feel uncomfortable. If you say you don't eat meat because you're sensitive to the mistreatment of livestock animals, but then accept a steak at your family barbecue reunion, you'll most likely feel uncomfortable after being inconsistent in your actions.

The law of consistency refers to your audience's need to keep their commitments. For example, if you ask your audience whether they would buy a certain product if you created it for them, the ones who answer "yes" may feel the obligation to be consistent and commit to their word by buying the product once it's released.

4. Liking

"People prefer to say 'yes' to those they know and like," Cialdini says.

That's kind of obvious. Would you buy a product, a painting, or a coaching session from someone you dislike, if someone you liked better offered an equivalent? Probably not. The question, then, is how do we make people like us? According to Cialdini's research, we tend to like people:

- **Who are similar to us**
  Share our values, background, current situation, etc.
- **Who cooperate with us in a common goal**
  Work with us as a team, or share our vision.
- **Who have complimented us**
  Who make us feel good about ourselves.

Dave Kerpen, author of *Likeable Business*, states that what is critical in building a following is to first make sure that people know you, second, that they like you, and third, that they trust you.

Liking is at the center of building relationships, and for it to happen, people need to know you and connect with you. Then, to become followers or customers, they also need to trust you. There is no shortcut for this.

Here is where knowing your audience well and feeling empathy for them will be particularly handy. If you can demonstrate to your audience that you understand their situation because you've *also* been there and remember how it was, they'll feel a deeper connection to you. They'll relate to you.

People who share your values will also connect with you more easily. They'll see what you stand for by reading your organization's mission statement or hearing your elevator pitch and tagline, and those who feel touched and concerned about your vision will more easily become buyers of your products and services.

You also should tell your audience that you will be working with them towards achieving their goals, and that their well-being is also your concern.

Plus, giving genuine compliments on their improvements, the choices they made, and their perseverance can also boost your likeability, as you'll make them feel good about themselves.

5. Social Proof and Consensus

Cialdini says, "Especially when they are uncertain, people will look for actions of others to determine their own."

We usually feel better making a decision if others have made the same choice or taken the same action. It validates our behavior and makes us feel more confident that we made the right decision.

Also, it's been shown that people trust recommendations from peers more than from any other sources. According to a study by Nielsen[7] in 2009:

> "Recommendations from personal acquaintances or opinions posted by consumers online are the most trusted forms of advertising. Ninety percent of consumers surveyed noted that they trust recommendations from people they know, while 70 percent trusted consumer opinions posted online."

This means that people will be keener and feel more reassured about buying your product if they see that others have also bought it, and even more so if other buyers have expressed their satisfaction and written a great product review.

Therefore, adding testimonials from real buyers to your website—especially on the product sales page—should have a positive impact on the number of sales.

Another way you can make people more comfortable with buying your product is to highlight the popular items. You can tell them what the most popular choice is, or simply mention how many people have purchased the product.

The law of social proof and consensus also affects social sharing and liking. People are usually keener on sharing content that has already been shared by others and liking a page that is very popular (has many fans).

---

[7] Study Nielsen http://www.nielsen.com/us/en/insights/news/2009/global-advertising-consumers-trust-real-friends-and-virtual-strangers-the-most.html

6. Scarcity

Along with social proof, scarcity is probably the element that will help you the most in increasing sales.

Scarcity refers to a limited quantity of an offer. If your offer is a service, it's possible that there are limited places available, and this is very understandable. Scarcity is also very conceivable for a physical product—people can't order a product that's out of stock. In those cases, you can easily mention that people should register or buy as soon as possible, because availability is limited.

However, what about a digital product that can't really be physically *limited*?

For digital products like online courses or eBooks, you could offer bonus items for the first few purchases. Bonus items can be an audio version of your book, access to a higher level course, a one-on-one consulting session, or anything that is perceived as valuable by your audience.

You could also do a "flash sale." For example, you could send an email to previous buyers to offer them your new product at 30% off for a limited time as a launch special. Note that it is wise not to overuse the discount strategy.

More Persuasion Tips to Increase Your Product Sales

Address Objections

Objections are reasons why a potential buyer may hesitate on the purchase.

You'll convince your audience to buy your product or service more easily if you address their objections *before* they even have time to come up with them, by providing counterarguments to these objections.

Here are some examples of objections:

- "I don't know if I'll be able to create a website. I'm a real dummy with computers!"
- "I don't have time."
- "It's a little expensive for my budget."

Counterarguments:

- "I'll show you the whole process, step-by-step, in such a simple way that even your grandmother could do it!"
- "You can take the course at your own pace with only two hours per week. In two months, you'll know enough Spanish vocabulary and verbs to speak to the hotel staff on your vacation."
- "Using your new skill acquired from the course, you will recover your investment within two weeks."

Objections are usually related to time, money, or confidence in whether the product will help them solve their problem or satisfy their needs.

Note that using *your audience's* expressions and language style when mentioning the objections will work best.

The Loss and the Gain

You must also mention what people will gain by consuming your products (benefits), or even what they'll lose by not doing so.

Here's an example:

A fitness trainer sells exercise and nutrition programs through his website. Some of the benefits his target audience will gain after purchasing and using his program are:

- Lowering their cholesterol level
- Lowering their blood pressure
- Gaining more energy
- Sleeping better
- Having a greater ability to focus
- Being in a better mood
- Feeling better in their own skin
- Increasing their life expectancy

The loss, then, is almost opposite to the gain:

- Feeling tired and not having the energy to play with the kids
- Being at risk for heart disease, diabetes, and other dangerous health conditions
- Suffering from insomnia
- Being impatient and moody, which may affect relationships

Marketer Derek Halpern (*SocialTriggers.com*) says there are two types of motivational focus: **prevention focus** and **promotion focus**.

People who are more of the "prevention" type tend to be more sensitive towards what they could lose. They want to be safe. As for people who are more of the "promotion" type, they will be more sensitive to what they could gain, or to opportunities.

On a product sales page, you should use both "loss" and "gain" motivation tactics, since the page will be promoting to a large number of people of potentially both types.

Offer a Good Guarantee

A guarantee lowers the buyer's anxiety. It diminishes the doubts the customer might have about purchasing by knowing that, if he isn't satisfied with the product, he can get a full refund within the following week or month.

If you think that offering such guarantees will make you lose money because some people will ask for a refund, don't worry. First, if you offer a good guarantee, a *lot* more people will buy your product. Second, if your product is good, very few will ask for a refund.

Use Persuasion Techniques on Your About Page

The primary goal of your About page isn't to generate sales, but it is a great place to use some of the persuasion principles to increase your influence.

Here's how to use them:

Liking

Contrary to popular belief, the About page isn't mainly about *you*, your story, credentials, and expertise. Yes, you should mention them at some point on your About page, but the first few paragraphs of this section of your website should be about *them*—your audience. You must answer the big question they'll have: "What's in it for me?"

You should begin by showing empathy and letting them know that you understand their situation (be specific and name the situation).

All of this should be done using their language—words and expressions.

You should mention that you've been in their situation before, so they feel that you're "one of them."

Genuinely state that you want to help them achieve their goal, and that this is the purpose of your website. By doing so, you start building a trusting relationship with your audience. The right people (your ideal customers) will connect with you because they'll see that you are similar to them and that you want to work with them to achieve their goals.

The approach you take in writing your About page will differ depending on your industry and on the product or service you're offering.

Just remember, it has to be about *them* first. People are self-centered. Clearly mention what's in it for them using an empathic approach.

Reciprocation

You can give more details about what they'll find on your website. If there's a blog, tell them about the valuable content you'll be providing on a consistent basis.

Mention the great tips and the helpful information they'll get through your site. They'll be grateful for your help, and, hopefully, have this in mind when you promote a paid product.

Credibility

Now you can insert your credentials.

Reassure your audience that you're the ideal person to serve them by showing your expertise on the topic – your experience in the field and your credentials. Mention the elements that will support your position of authority, like:

- Education
- Work
- Other experiences

Social Proof

If you have a considerable following on social media, you can display your content count for likes and shares by using the Facebook like box. You could also add social proof facts, such as: "More than fifty people have had excellent results using our service" or "Subscribe to our email list and join a community of more than 10,000 members."

If your site is new and you don't have much of a following or many subscribers (or any at all), you could ask someone you know who has benefited from your product or service to write a testimonial, which you can display at the end of your About page or in the right sidebar.

With only a few tweaks to your About page, you'll inspire trust from your audience, which is a primary requirement for them to become customers.

What to Remember About Persuasion

1) If you have a sincere desire to serve your audience and genuinely believe they can benefit from your product or service, using persuasion isn't unethical.

2) Robert Cialdini's field research on persuasion has been the reference on the topic for many years. It explains the six main principles of persuasion:

- Reciprocation
- Credibility
- Commitment and consistency
- Social proof and consensus
- Liking
- Scarcity

3) The two main sections of your website where you should apply these persuasion techniques are your Sales page and your About page.

4) Along with the persuasion principles on your Sales page, you should:
- Mention the gain (benefits) of consuming your product, and the loss (what your audience would be missing) by not doing so.
- Address objections people may have and provide counterarguments.
- Offer a good guarantee to demonstrate the trust you have in your own product and diminish your potential customers' purchase anxiety.

5) Your About page is a great place to connect with your audience, build trust and rapport, and introduce yourself as the ideal person to help them.

Take Action

(Suggested time to allow for the exercise: 3 hours)

1) Create a good Sales page.
   - Use the six principles of persuasion. For scarcity, think of bonus items you could offer for a limited time or for the first few buyers to add a sense of urgency.
   - Write down the objections your potential customers may have and find the counterarguments.
   - Write down the benefits (what buyers would gain) of using your product, and what they would lose or miss out on by not doing so.
   - Think of a great guarantee you could give.

2) Create a good About page.
Use the persuasion principles of:
   - **Liking**
   State "what's in it" for your audience, and explain how you are similar to them. Show understanding, empathy, and a genuine desire to serve.
   - **Reciprocation**
   What great value do you provide that they will really appreciate?
   - **Credibility**
   What demonstrates your position of authority on the topic and in the field? Why are you the best person to help them?
   - **Social proof**
   Mention that others have used your product or service or have subscribed to your email list, liked your Facebook page, etc. Get a few testimonials from satisfied customers and display them on the page.

CHAPTER 12

GETTING FEEDBACK THROUGH TESTING

Split Testing

Over time, I've noticed a common trait among people who achieve great success with their online business—they like tests.

They do a lot of what we call "split testing" or "A/B testing." We've already mentioned A/B testing in Chapter 7. A split test means experimenting with two versions of something to see which one results in the best conversion rate.

A conversion rate is the percentage of your visitors who achieve a given goal, a goal that *you* had predetermined—for example, subscribing to your email list, buying your product or downloading a document.

What can be tested includes an opt-in form's layout, a headline or a call-to-action button, a squeeze page image, an advertising campaign, etc.

What happens is that half of the visitors to your website will see Version A, and the other half will see Version B. You'll observe the conversion results of each version, keep the one that converts best, and discard the other.

Note that all of this is done through an analytics tool. You could then create a third version to test it against the first winner and continue this process by always keeping what converts best. This way, you could end up with a version that converts ten times better than the first one you created, meaning that you would gain ten times more email subscribers, generate ten times more sales, or get ten times more coaching clients.

I guess you understand why successful people online are usually the ones who conduct a lot of tests. Basically, they continually tweak everything they do to improve and optimize their message or offer.

What to Test

Did you ever think that modifying a single word in an opt-in form could make a significant difference? Well, it does. One word can make more people click on a button than another word.

Note that it's important to test only *one* aspect at a time, or you won't know exactly which variable made a difference.

1. Opt-in Forms

These are the forms used to collect your website visitors' emails. You can experiment with different types of forms, using different sizes, colors, or images. The text and the call-to-action button are probably the most important. For example, if the free gift you offer to email subscribers is a list of five exercises to build upper body muscles, then you could experiment with these two headlines:

Version A) "Build upper body muscles—5 effective exercises"

Version B) "Build upper body muscles—See a difference within 3 weeks"

An example of two calls to action:

Call-to-action Version A) Download Now

Call-to-action Version B) Get instant access

The location of the form on your web page can also impact the conversion rate. Analyze the locations that get better results.

2. Sales Page

Your product sales page is a squeeze page—a distraction-free page—that pitches your product to your audience.

Just like with the opt-in form, you want to test different variations of the headline, the text that mentions the benefits, the choice of images, font and colors, and the call to action. You could even test the objections and the way you address them (counterarguments).

3. Opt-in Freebie

As your current main objective is to build an email list, you should experiment with everything you can, to get as many email subscribers as possible.

You should also test different freebie offers to identify what your audience is most interested in getting. Not only will you build your list faster, but it's also a great way to have an idea of which paid product you should eventually offer. Experiment with:

- **The freebie format**
  Are there more people subscribing for an email series, a video, a cheat sheet or checklist, or an eBook?

- **The freebie topic**
  For example, a site about personal development could experiment with different opt-in freebies, such as an eBook on body language, one on becoming more charismatic and another about self-confidence, to determine which is most popular among site visitors.

4. Email Marketing

You can conduct split testing within your email campaigns by trying different:

- **Email subject lines**

  Experiment with different email subject lines to see which leads to the highest open rate. MailChimp data[8] shows that the subject lines that get the best open rates are pretty straightforward and don't look like advertising. Some of the keywords that seem to do best in the subject lines are: posts, jobs, survey, weeks and e-newsletter.

- **Sender's name**

  Test if you get a better open rate when using your personal name or your company's name.

- **Frequency**

  Experiment with the frequency of the emails you send to your subscriber list. For example, send daily emails to Segment A and weekly emails to Segment B.

- **Day of the week and time of day**

  You can also test different days of the week and times of day. For my lists, I've noticed a higher open rate from Tuesday to Thursday, early in the morning. It may be different for you, depending on your field of activity. This is the type of information you will only get through experimenting.

---

[8] MailChimp data: http://mailchimp.com/resources/research/email-marketing-subject-line-comparison/

- **Click-through rate**

    If you send emails containing links to click, for example to read a blog post or get access to another resource, not only will you want to test the email opening rate, but also the click-through rate. How many people who open the email actually click on the link in the message?

    The click-through rate can be impacted by the day and time you send the email, and also by the nature of the resource you're sharing. Therefore, you could test different recommendations for tools and resources, and see which sparks the most interest.

5. Pricing

I wouldn't necessarily recommend that you experiment by offering your product at different prices, since this could lead to discontent from members of your audience who end up noticing it. However, you could test different *ways* to mention the same price. For example, a $30/month membership could be:

- $360/year
- $30/month
- $7/week
- $1/day

6. Advertising Campaigns

You must also use testing to lower your cost of lead acquisition (cost per subscriber or per product sale) in your advertising campaigns, or your campaigns might not be profitable. With too high a cost of acquisition, you'll lose money.

By tweaking your ads' templates and copy, you'll diminish your lead acquisition cost and optimize your return on investment by gaining more customers or subscribers at the lowest possible cost.

Tools to Conduct Tests

Facebook Ads

Facebook advertising is one of the greatest tools to split test just about anything. You can create two ad versions within the same campaign to test a headline, an image or a call-to-action. You can even test different target audiences.

The system can even automatically remove the version that converts least and only keep the best one to ensure better results. You should keep track of your campaign closely and test several versions, one after the other, against the winner. With just a slight tweak, you may see a considerable difference in the return on investment of your campaign.

Jon Haws, author and entrepreneur (*Nrsng.com*), said that a simple tweak in the lightening effect of an image once led to a difference of 35 cents in lead acquisition cost. This is huge! One ad version cost him 5 cents per lead, and the other cost 40 cents. You would obviously want to take the latter down as fast as possible.

Experiment with (among others):

- The image
- The headline
- The text (body)
- The call-to-action
- The target audience
- Targeting mobile versus desktop users
- The day of the week and time of day

Even without selling a product, you could still use Facebook Ads to test the title or the cover of a book that you will publish, an opt-in freebie, a webinar topic, or anything else to know what triggers more interest. It's a great tool to get feedback from your target audience.

Google AdWords

We've already explained that there are organic search results and paid ones. The sponsored ones are the first shown on top and on the right-side column of the results page. Google AdWords is the program that puts sponsored links on Google's search results page. It's a pay-per-click system, meaning that the advertiser is charged every time a person clicks on the link.

In 2006, Tim Ferriss tested several titles and subtitles for his book *The 4-Hour Workweek* using a Google AdWords campaign. He determined the best title to use for his book according to the number of clicks it got. The one that was getting the most engagement (clicks) was more promising.

Many other entrepreneurs have used the same tactic. However, AdWords can be expensive, and unless you take the time to learn how to use it well, I recommend starting with Facebook advertising or another method first.

Email Marketing Service Provider

We mentioned earlier that one feature you should be looking for when selecting an email marketing service provider is the ability to conduct A/B testing.

A good email marketing service will allow you to segment your list and split test different opt-in forms and email campaigns.

Squeeze Pages and Opt-in Forms

Landing page builders such as *LeadPages.com* or *InstaPages.com* include a split testing feature. The same goes for several opt-in form providers, such as *OptinMonster.com* and *ThriveThemes.com/leads*.

Google Analytics

Once your website is live, you should register an account with Google Analytics. It's a free tool from Google that provides insights about your visitor demographics, the daily or monthly number of visits to your site, the peak time for visits, the sources of traffic, etc. This is essential information for your business.

Another feature in your Google Analytics account is called "Content Experiments." With this feature, you can experiment with different (up to six) versions of a page to test which converts best. This is a great way to test sales pages, for example.

I've created a document that explains the steps to follow to set up your Google Analytics account and install the related plugin on your website. You can find this document in the bonus material section.

The bottom line is that conducting tests will allow you to get more subscribers, make more sales, and grow your business faster.

What to Remember for Testing

1) Most successful online business owners conduct a lot of tests.

2) Testing will help you gain more subscribers, generate more sales, and grow your business faster.

3) You can test just about anything, but the most common elements to test are:
- Opt-in forms
- Opt-in freebies
- Landing (squeeze) pages
- Email campaigns
- Advertising campaigns

You can make changes to the headlines, images, layout, text, calls-to-action, the benefits of your product, objections and counterarguments, etc.

4) To conduct experiments, you need analytic tools such as:
- Google Analytics—Content Experiments
- An email marketing service provider
- Facebook Ad Manager
- Google AdWords
- A landing page builder and opt-in form services

5) Test only one element at a time.

Take Action

(Suggested time to allow for the exercise: 2 hours)

1) Test an opt-in form

In your email marketing software, create two versions of an opt-in form (to collect emails) using the A/B testing feature. Only test one element at a time—the call-to-action button, the headline, the image or the text. Conduct such tests for different elements of your form. Observe, over time, which results in more conversions.

2) Test your landing pages

Using the same method as the opt-in form, test the conversion of your landing pages (for example, your product sales page).

3) Facebook Ads

When you advertise on Facebook, make sure to create different ads per campaign, tweaking the main elements one at a time. Observe and keep the version that is converting best.

CHAPTER 13

OUTSOURCING

There are two main benefits to outsourcing some of your activities as your business grows: one is to avoid becoming overwhelmed, and the other is to increase your income.

As your business grows, the workload will get heavier. Because there are only so many hours in a day, an ideal solution to get more done without getting exhausted is to delegate some of your activities. Once your business starts generating revenue, it's smart to hire a virtual assistant to help you with simple but time-consuming tasks, even for just a few hours per week. You could then concentrate your energy on more valuable aspects of your business.

For example, at some point, you might want to build a presence on more social media platforms. However, will you really spend two hours a day creating content and searching for images and quotes to publish on those different social platforms? It would be a good idea to outsource these tasks and focus on the most lucrative activities of your business.

Some tasks that are easy to delegate include:

- Searching for images for your articles
- Editing and formatting the articles and the images
- Researching information
- Creating content for social media. For example, using an article you have written to create a SlideShare presentation, an image to pin on Pinterest and one to publish on Instagram, and a quote to tweet.

Of course, the tasks will differ depending on your business. The main point to understand is that by trying to do everything yourself, you might end up burned out, which won't help you or your business.

Another benefit to outsourcing part of your activities is that you'll increase your income. By delegating the less lucrative tasks, you'll have more time to focus on the higher paid ones and therefore increase your revenue.

Marketer Perry Marshall states that we can divide everything we do into $10-per-hour, $100-per-hour, and $1000-per-hour (etc.) tasks. He explains that "you can increase your income by focusing on the activities that are worth $100 or $1000-per-hour, and finding other ways to get the lowest value activities done—like hiring someone to do it for you."

Some entrepreneurs will naturally delegate part of their activities that they judge to be less important to create space in their schedule for higher value tasks. Others have the tendency to want to do everything themselves, perhaps to stay in control and make sure it's done correctly. That being said, if you study the strategies of successful entrepreneurs, you'll probably notice that there are two main elements that distinguish them from others:

- o They test everything instead of assuming (preceding chapter).
- o They delegate what can be done by others.

These two strategies can really make a difference in your business growth and in the income you'll generate.

When you are ready to delegate part of your activities, you can hire a personal assistant for ongoing assistance, or freelancers for short-term jobs.

There are platforms and agencies that can facilitate the process of finding someone that is a good fit for your needs, such as *VirtualStaffFinder.com*, *TasksEveryday.com* and *LongerDays.com*. You can also look at freelancing sites, like *Upwork.com*, *Guru.com* or *Freelancer.com*.

I would also recommend the book *Virtual Freedom* by Chris Ducker, which is a step-by-step guide for entrepreneurs who wish to work with virtual employees.

What to Remember About Outsourcing

1) There are two main benefits to outsourcing some of your activities as your business grows:

- o Avoid becoming overwhelmed
- o Increase your income

2) By delegating the less lucrative tasks, you'll have more time to focus on the higher-paying ones and therefore increase your revenue.

Take Action

(Suggested time to allow for the exercise: 1 hour)

1) Make a list of your business activities (tasks)

2) For each task, determine:

- What is its value? ($/hour)
  Is it a $10/h, a $100/h or a $1000 or more/hour task?
  Ask yourself: What value does this specific task bring to the market?

- Are you the only person who can handle it, or can it be delegated?
  Separate the tasks according to whether only you can handle them, or if someone else could take care of them. For example, if you are a coach, only you can coach your clients. However, you could outsource online marketing, social media content creation, or almost any other administrative task.

- What do you enjoy most and least doing?
  Some of your daily tasks might feel like a pain. If someone other than yourself can handle them, outsource!

WHAT'S NEXT?

In the preceding chapters, we discussed the main concepts to consider when starting an online business. The formula to build a successful business isn't very complicated. You should:

1. Select a topic you're interested in and a niche market you want to serve.
2. Find your chosen market's "pain."
3. Determine the best solution (product) to their problem, and package it in a format that will be well received by your audience.
4. Position your solution (product) well by clearly stating who it is (and isn't) for, by differentiating it from the other offers on the market, and by pricing it properly.
5. Clearly communicate your offer by mentioning its benefits.
6. Conduct tests to validate your hypothesis and then adjust and improve your offer to better serve your market.
7. Delegate and outsource some of your tasks.

Trying to cut corners in this process would mean wasting time in the end. No matter what, at some point, you'll have to address every aspect of this process.

But is that everything you need to start a business?

Well, no, not exactly. You need, more than anything, to take action. Questions you might have will only be answered once you get to work!

First, you'll have to make room in your schedule.

How many hours per week should you be working on your business? Well, there is no magic number. The more time you put into your project, the faster you'll likely see results. I would say that you should spend at least enough hours to build a habit—around one hour per day, at least. If you can allow 20 hours per week—let's say eight hours on the weekend and two and a half hours every weekday—that's even better. It all depends on your personal situation.

It's true that starting an online business can feel overwhelming. Yes, there will be many things to do, and many ideas will be occupying your mind, but it's important to take it step-by-step, and not to try to do everything at the same time. This book gave you a step-by-step framework that you can follow to help you.

We have mentioned the importance of being curious and thirsty to learn—to take classes, listen to podcasts and attend conferences.

However, it's better to avoid an information overload and to learn about each concept as you apply it, as you take action. If you are at the stage of finding your niche market, then listening to podcast episodes about growing your social media following wouldn't be helpful—you don't need that information at that precise moment, and you probably won't remember all the information when you eventually need it.

Learn only what you can apply *right now*.

Overcoming Doubt

Even with the Internet helping to make it much easier to become an entrepreneur, there will still be some roadblocks along the way.

One of the main obstacles you'll encounter will be your mindset: your own doubts and limiting beliefs. Doubts are part of the process and are inevitable. At times, you'll find yourself wondering if you have chosen the right path, and whether you're being a fool by trying to become an entrepreneur. You'll doubt your idea and even your skills. This is normal, and it happens to everyone.

You may even find that some of your peers and family members don't understand your project and don't give you the support you were expecting from them. If this happens, don't get upset. Instead, you must find the strength of character to keep going. That's one of the main reasons why it's so important to surround yourself with the best people to help you move forward, by creating a mastermind group, finding mentors and attending Meetup events in your city, as a way to meet other entrepreneurs. Essentially, you'll need to build your own support circle.

Also, to help you move forward with your business, always keep in mind your vision—your larger goal—and your "why."

HAVE YOU ENJOYED THIS BOOK?

This book was essentially a collection of information that has helped me in my own digital journey. I sincerely hope that it has been useful to you as well. I have personally found, within the online world, fulfillment and satisfaction, and I wish you the same.

If you've enjoyed this book and found it useful, I'd be sincerely grateful if you would post a review. Your support really does make all the difference, and it would mean a lot to me if you took the time. I read all my reviews and greatly appreciate your feedback.

Finally, don't forget to claim your workbook and other bonus material (see next page).

Thank you for reading!

BONUS MATERIAL

Are included with this book:

- Workbook
- Book Summary
- *Building Authority and Credibility* (PDF)
- Guide to Setting up HostGator and WordPress.org
- Guide to Setting up Google Analytics
- List Of WordPress Plugins
- Other Useful Resources

You can download them at:

www.BecomeOnlineEntrepreneur.com/online-business-book-bonus/

COMPLEMENTARY READING

GETTING THE RIGHT MINDSET

The ONE Thing: The Surprisingly Simple Truth Behind Extraordinary Results, by Gary Keller and Jay Papasan

PRODUCT VALIDATION

Will It Fly? How to Test Your Next Business Idea So You Don't Waste Your Time and Money, by Pat Flynn

PRODUCT LAUNCH

Launch: An Internet Millionaire's Secret Formula To Sell Almost Anything Online, Build A Business You Love, And Live The Life Of Your Dreams, by Jeff Walker

MARKETING

80/20 Sales and Marketing: The Definitive Guide to Working Less and Making More, by Perry Marshall

GUIDE TO OUTSOURCING

Virtual Freedom: How to Work with Virtual Staff to Buy More Time, Become More Productive, and Build Your Dream Business, by Chris Ducker

Printed in Great Britain
by Amazon